ALSO BY TOM BROKAW

The Greatest Generation

THE

GREATEST

GENERATION

SPEAKS

.

I Remember

I Remember

·

WHAT I REMEMBER
MOST ABOUT THE WAR YEARS

MILITARY UNIT, JOB

THE BEST MOMENT

I Remember

MY LONGEST DAY

BEST FRIENDS

I Remember

·
————————

WHEN THE WAR WAS OVER

_____

_____

_____

_____

_____

_____

_____

_____

_____

_____

_____

_____

_____

WHAT I MISS ABOUT THAT TIME

_____

_____

_____

_____

_____

_____

_____

_____

_____

_____

_____

_____

_____

_____

_____

I Remember

•

MY PHOTOGRAPHS

TOM BROKAW

·

THE GREATEST GENERATION SPEAKS

·

Letters and Reflections

RANDOM HOUSE
LARGE PRINT

A Division of Random House, Inc.
Published in Association with Random House
New York 1999

The Library of Congress has established a cataloging-in-
publication record for this title.

ISBN 0-375-40922-X

Random House Web Address:
http://www.randomhouse.com/

Printed in the United States of America

FIRST LARGE PRINT EDITION

Title-page photo: UPI/Corbis-Bettmann

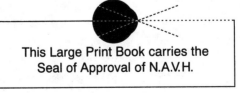

**This Large Print Book carries the
Seal of Approval of N.A.V.H.**

To the men and women
of the greatest generation
with gratitude and admiration

ACKNOWLEDGMENTS

This is a book crafted by many memories, youthful insights, and the wisdom that come with seasons of despair and triumph. It is, most of all, another tribute to the men and women who rode the treacherous currents and sailed with the fair winds of most of the twentieth century.

It would not have been possible to have produced this book without the tireless and enthusiastic assistance of a remarkable group of young women who are making their own mark of greatness at an early age:

Elizabeth Bowyer, who was indispensable in assisting me with *The Greatest Generation,* reenlisted for this book, working late nights and odd hours while she held down a summer job at a prestigious New York law firm and studied at Columbia Law School. I am in awe of her ability to do so many tasks so well simultaneously. I am also grateful for her personal passion about this subject.

Catherine Balsam-Schwaber and Tara Pepper of NBC News were invaluable in their roles as readers, researchers, and organizers. No matter how large the stack of new mail or how difficult the research project, they went about their assignments with quiet efficiency and good cheer.

My friend Frank Gannon read the manuscript (as he did the manuscript of *The Greatest Generation*) and made several helpful suggestions for which I am very grateful.

As she did with *The Greatest Generation*, Erin O'Connor managed to keep my NBC News responsibilities, author's role, and personal life in balance and mostly on schedule. She knows when to say yes and how to say no without offending anyone, including me (although she is wisely trying to get me to say no more often). I am forever in your debt, Erin.

At Random House, my peerless editor and great friend, Kate Medina, cheered me on while gently and thoughtfully steering the book from start to finish. She is a brave and brilliant inspiration.

Her assistant, Meaghan Rady, has an editor's eye and the cool of an air-traffic controller. She kept *The Greatest Generation Speaks* from crash-landing on any number of occasions. She also makes me laugh with her impish sense of humor.

The other members of the Random House team who performed so gracefully under the enormous pressure of looming deadlines are Benjamin Dreyer, Carole Lowenstein, Jolanta Benal, Evan Stone, Maria Massey, Andy Carpenter, and Richard Elman. Thank you all.

The real authors of this book deserve the greatest accolades: the men and women, young and old, who shared their stories, their tears, their gentle criticisms, and their quiet pride in lives lived well. There is no single American voice, but the chorus is thrilling.

The stories that you will read here have been edited and they are reprinted with the permission of the authors. We have attempted to verify all of the factual information, but in some cases these are memories and impressions more than a half-century old.

The selection process was difficult because there were so many letters and memoirs. I am deeply grateful to all who wrote, and I treasure each of the stories. They widen and enrich the family portrait I wanted to present in *The Greatest Generation.*

To be sure, there are stories that I missed, and for that I accept full responsibility. I hope they will find audiences in family gatherings, schools, community celebrations, barrooms, and churches. They are too important, too instructive, and too entertaining to be cloistered forever.

CONTENTS

INTRODUCTION

I am a child of the American men and women who grew up in the Great Depression, who came of age in World War II and then devoted their adult years to the building of modern America—the remarkable people I wrote about in *The Greatest Generation*. As I walked the beaches of Normandy on the fortieth and fiftieth anniversaries of D-Day, I first began to fully realize how they had shaped my life. They were my parents and the parents of my friends, teachers, ministers, physicians, and hometown merchants, the men and women who showed me the way through their own exacting standards of hard work, sacrifice, and personal responsibility. I began to understand how much I owed them.

As a son of working-class parents who

were deeply rooted in the harsh economic realities of the Depression and the common challenges of the war, I reflected on the good fortune of my generation and the world we inherited. So many of us were the first in our families to attend college and to find that good jobs were plentiful. My generation and those that followed took their place in a world of broader horizons and expanded rights for women and ethnic minorities.

It wasn't a perfect world, of course.

Far too many of my contemporaries died in Vietnam, but others gave birth to long-overdue political and social change. The excesses of youthful rebellion in the sixties and seventies were painful, even destructive in some aspects, but the foundation of the country and its complex culture withstood the onslaught and remained secure. Moreover, my generation and those that followed were not judged by their excesses alone; indeed, we were given more opportunities in more arenas than our parents had dared to dream.

A few years ago, when I thought about my own good fortune in life and career, somehow it seemed inadequate to thank just my parents, even though their help was irreplaceable and enduring. There were so many people in the fabric of my life as I grew up who influenced me—teachers and ministers, coaches and merchants, the mothers and fathers of my friends—all men and women who had experienced great hardship during the Depression and the war years.

When I set out to write *The Greatest Generation,* I was inspired by these people and by the realization that my world of endless possibilities, despite all its imperfections, was the work of these men and women. By writing their stories, I had finally found a way to say thank you. I wanted that book to be my gift to them, an expression of admiration and gratitude for all they had achieved, and for the legacy they passed on to future generations.

Of course, I hoped that the book would be well received by the people about whom I was writing. As for younger generations, I wasn't sure what to expect. So many of the people I talked with from the World War II generation told me their kids weren't much interested in hearing about the Depression, the war, the sacrifices of the fifties. As for their grandchildren—a generation coming of age in a time of personal computers, digital video, and unprecedented prosperity—to them, stories about the Great Depression and World War II were like grainy black-and-white images in dusty schoolbooks or on late-night television. Wouldn't stories about people's lives during the 1930s, 1940s, and 1950s seem like ancient history to a thirtysomething or to a teenager shaping a life for America and the world in the twenty-first century?

And so the enthusiastic response to *The Greatest Generation* has been not only a pleasant surprise, but also deeply gratifying in ways I could never have predicted. From what people say to me on the street and write in letters, some of which appear in this book, *The Greatest Generation* seems to have inspired within many families, communities, schools, and even corners of the political arena a reevaluation of the past, and a dialogue about the core values of that time and of the present.

Children and grandchildren of the Greatest Generation are telling me they now understand the values reflected in the lives of the people they know from the World War II era, values that to many may have seemed a little tiresome in these more permissive times—the older generation's strict code of conduct and discipline; their frugality; and their expectation that once the teenage years were over, the serious grown-up years would begin.

My favorite reaction to *The Greatest Generation,* however, is expressed to me in unexpected moments—on a ski slope, in an airport, on a street in New York, in the Pentagon. Men about my age—cops, business executives, military men, construction workers—grab my hand, look me in the eye, and say, "I read your book. Thank you for helping me understand my father." Then they turn and walk away.

Any journalist would be flattered to have his or her work become a catalyst for reflection and examination, but I have no illusion about my personal role in all this. I was merely the reporter, the vehicle for people's stories and the lessons they contained. So many of the veterans said of their service during the war, "It was an honor," and I feel in turn it was an honor to have written about the people in that book.

I was totally unprepared for the avalanche of letters that appeared as soon as *The Greatest Generation* was published. Members of that generation, and their children, sent moving stories about the heroism, values, friendships, and pain of those times, and of the effect the book and its memories of the Depression and World War II had on their lives today. I wrote a book about America, and a lot of America is writing back.

The letters, many of them written in firm Palmer penmanship on flowered stationery, made me reflect further on the meaning of those difficult times. I also thought the letters contained wisdom, and valuable lessons about life, and were of value as history too. Members of the Greatest Generation still believe in the old-fashioned virtues of letter writing and personal testimony. Some of them could also draw on letters they had sent or received back then, letters written during the war, from the front lines to people back home, or from families to their loved ones in harm's way in distant places.

In these pages, you'll hear directly from the Greatest Generation and their children; you'll hear voices and more stories, as the Greatest Generation and their families speak out, some for the first time. Many of them say they felt they had no audience until now. You'll also hear how the dialogue sparked by the book caused younger generations to reexamine their own lives and values, with a fresh perspective.

Most of the letters you'll find here arrived unsolicited. Some I requested, hoping to fill in some gaps and oversights. Even so, I know there are many more voices, experiences, stories; we've included some pages here for you to write your own.

If we are to heed the past to prepare for the future, we should listen to these voices of a generation that speaks to us of duty and honor, sacrifice and accomplishment. I hope more of their stories will be preserved and cherished as reminders of all that we owe them and all that we can learn from them.

I
____•____

WAR
STORIES

Frames of motion-picture war coverage taken by Raymond Daum, somewhere on the Roer River, Germany, 1942–43.

Recently I read again Erich Maria Remarque's classic war novel *All Quiet on the Western Front*. It is a German soldier's reflection on the terror, cruelty, and absurdity of combat during World War I, yet the themes perfectly matched what American veterans wrote in their personal accounts of life at the front during World War II.

Those memoirs, many of them self-published or simply bound manuscripts, add to the rich body of literature from World War II. The best of that literature—the works of James Jones, Norman Mailer, Kurt Vonnegut, William Manchester, Joseph Heller, and Paul Fussell, for example—is well known. The homespun books will likely never be read outside the authors' immediate families. Still, the memoirs of infantrymen, fliers, sailors, and chaplains get at the essential truths of war in their own memorable and deeply personal fashion. They also remind us that for these men, in their late teens and early twenties, the lessons of death, fate, futility, and pure, unalloyed high-risk adventure were never to be matched in their other experiences.

Whenever an American flier was downed during the NATO bombing raids on Serbia, he was quickly located and picked up by elite search-and-rescue units utilizing the latest high-technology communications systems, which made it possible for the operation to be monitored thousands of miles away, in the Pentagon. In contrast, consider the Americans who were trapped by the Japanese on Corregidor in the Philippines at the outset of World War II. One of them was Clarence M. Graham, now eighty years old and living on a small landholding in Oregon. He was taken prisoner at the beginning of May 1942, and shipped off to Japan to work in a coal mine across the bay from a city called Nagasaki. For the next three and a half years he worked in the mine and then, one day in the summer of 1945, he was witness to a historic event.

This is what he wrote to me.

I am just one of many who were engaged in that war (WWII). I was stationed in the Philippines when it started and in an anti-aircraft battery. We were on the Bataan Peninsula. We were engaged in jungle fighting to the bitter end of that battle. Our battery escaped on the last night and made it back to the island of Corregidor. There we continued the defense until, on May 9th, 1942, Corregidor was captured. Nearly all of us who had survived to that point were undernourished and wounded in one way or another and most were wounded more than once.

We were taken prisoners by the Japanese and were used as slaves, tortured in various ways and maintained on starvation rations. Many were murdered. Many died of diseases and starvation. During the last year of three and a half years as a POW I worked in a condemned lateral of the Fukuoka coal mine near the city of Omuta, Japan. While there I was an eyewitness to the explosion of the atomic bomb that was dropped on the city of Nagasaki, just west and across the bay from us.

In a telephone interview, Graham took us back to the 1940s and his life in the coal mine.

It was very hot work, and very deep. The air was quite bad in there. The dust was terrible because it was a soft bituminous coal, and it filled the air and there were no currents and we had to breathe it. You had to keep your wits about you to stay alive because one false move, and your life was nothing in that country. They'd kill you in an instant if you disobeyed. . . .

In the mines, we had a shift that contained three types of work. There would be three or four men shoveling, three or four picking the coal off of the coal face, and the others would be picking up layers of slate and building pyramids of rock that hold up the ceiling. . . .

We took just one day at a time. I know that I kept saying, "I've got to keep my mind clear, and look for something good." Like . . . for one thing, I had a battery light that didn't leak on me and get acid on my skin. . . . Little things you'd keep yourself tantalized with, like . . . "Maybe soon you'll get a chance to get a break or something." . . .

I had a little belt on my waist, and all we wore was a loincloth. Sometimes I got to coughing so bad that I would take off my whole wardrobe and wrap it around my face so I could breathe. You could see only eyeballs and teeth when you looked at someone because they were covered with black coal. . . . We carried a cigar box with rice in it and that would be our ration for a twelve-hour shift. Sometimes the coal was so heavy we couldn't find our boxes. . . .

When you're a prisoner in those conditions, you don't care who it is, what his name is, who's next to you. You don't need a name. You have so little that you have to say, that you don't carry on a conversation. You're like oxen. . . . We always wondered [how the Allies were doing]. . . . Fellows made up rumors, but . . . we knew nothing. I kept thinking, well, if the Good Lord wanted me to get through this, I would make it. If he didn't, I wouldn't. I kept my faith pretty high, because so many just gave up. And you couldn't. You had to have inner drive, or you'd just die. . . .

We had just come in off of a long hard shift, and they were getting very brutal because . . . of the bombing on Hiroshima. And they were stirred up like hornets and taking it out on the Americans in the worst way. They said after Hiroshima they wouldn't give us any food, and that we would have to work until the Emperor decided that we didn't have to work anymore. We came out [of the mine] and it was daylight, and they didn't give us any breakfast. They told us to be quiet or we'd be killed. And then we had to go into our barracks—no talking. That's when . . . there was this air raid siren and we were ordered out to the trenches built in the camp between the barracks. They weren't trying to protect us [from the bombing]. . . . They needed our slave labor to get the coal to their war machines. No Japanese would go into the coal mines. . . .

We went in [to the trenches] and heard some planes but never saw them. . . . Then they blew the all clear. But just as we were coming out, I heard another plane and I looked up and saw an opening in the clouds, and I saw a B-29. I thought at the time, "Why don't they bomb, what are they joyriding for?" And then . . . we saw a brilliant flash— there's no way to describe the brightness. You couldn't tell where the flash came from—just brilliant brightness. Then seconds later there was a small tremor on the ground . . . you could feel the ground shaking. Then there was a strong wind that came from the west, which is the direction of Nagasaki, across the bay. And following that wind, there was a hot, hot wind.

Terribly hot. Hotter than direct sun on your face. Then there was a lull, and a terrific wind, almost a typhoon wind from the west, which was the air rushing back to the bomb center after the heat had gone up. The wind was so strong it toppled over some of our weak prisoners, just flattened them.

That's when we saw this huge orange dome to the west, and we were wondering what in the world it was. And then out of it, there was an opening about it and all the clouds disappeared and you could see the bright blue sky. And then this column of white smoke came up just like a tornado—a column. And we're standing there watching and the Japanese are all quiet. And then all of a sudden it starts to mushroom towards the top. . . . The funny thing about it all was that I never heard it. It must have been so loud that my ears were not able to pick it up. . . .

We were in a state of shock, not knowing anything about the atomic bomb. I remember someone saying,

"Wow, what a blast." Then someone else said, "They must have hit a big ammunition dump." Then after that we were ordered back to the barracks. They [the guards] were mean, but not as mean as after Hiroshima. Here, they were just in a state of shock. . . .

Six days later the war was over, and one of Graham's prison guards had an instant change of heart, saying to one of Graham's fellow prisoners, "You and I are now friends."

Graham didn't wait for a liberation force after all those years of misery, torture, and animal-like survival. He slipped through the fence, stole a bicycle, and made his way to the nearby city of Omuta to hook up with Allied forces.

He was flown out of Japan on a C-47, and as it gained altitude, he looked down to see a rainbow—a perfect circle against the deep blue waters of the China Sea. As he watched, a second rainbow formed around the first one. Graham, a lump in his throat, said to the pilot, "Do you see that?" The pilot responded, "Yes, it must be for you." Graham closed his eyes and offered a silent prayer to God. He was headed home.

ONE OF THE MOST HARROWING WAR stories involved American civilians who had the misfortune to sign on as the crew for a luxury cruise to the Far East just as the war broke out. June Behren's late husband, Hank, was a college student in Santa Barbara when he became a merchant seaman on the SS *President Harrison,* looking for a little adventure and college money for the following term.

This introduction to a Navy history of the *Harrison* affair by David and Gretchen Grover is a summary of what happened to the ship and crew.

In the fall of 1941 a voyage began routinely for the SS *President Harrison,* an American passenger liner departing San Francisco for the Far East. Passengers and crew were aware that their destination, although nominally still at peace, was a tense and unsettled part of the world. Nevertheless, they had no way of knowing that as they steamed toward the Orient, they were soon to be part of the opening act of a strange drama of war and captivity then beginning in the Pacific, or the Pacific theater, as, ironically, it was soon to be called. The *President Harrison* was never to know again the traditional completion of a ship's voyage: the ringing up of "Finished with Engines" on the engine order telegraph, and the beginning of a new set of pages in the logbook for the next voyage. Instead, after her heroic rescue of a Marine regiment from Shanghai she was destined to be captured by the Japanese while trying to rescue another detachment of U.S. Marines in North China from the threat of capture, then pressed into service as a Japanese troop ship, and subsequently sunk by an American submarine while transporting a load of Allied prisoners from Southeast Asia back to Japan.

Her crew was to spend three years and nine months—the entire period of American involvement in World War II—as prisoners of the Japanese, the first and largest group of merchant seamen to be so captured and the group that would spend as long in captivity as any other Americans during the war. Sixteen of her crew would not come back at all—some victims of the *Harrison*'s attempt to avoid capture, and others victims of the hardships of captivity.

Only fleeting references to the saga of the *President Harrison* and her crew appear in naval histories of World War II and in the virtually nonexistent maritime histories of that war. Her capture a few hours after Pearl Harbor received only passing notice in the press. Even after the war, most of the limited recognition she received posthumously was as a Japanese ship and as a suspect in the disappearance of an anthropological treasure.

Mrs. Behrens updates the story with her account of what happened to her husband.

My husband skipped out on his fall semester at Santa Barbara State College. He had worked summers on the *Lurline,* a cruise ship sailing between Los Angeles and Honolulu. The run to the Orient in 1941 would provide money for the school year.

An incredible story followed over the next four years. The true account reads like an adventure thriller. After the war and his return home in 1945, Hank's wartime experiences did not entitle him to GI benefits. He worked his way through college, and did not qualify for a GI housing loan.

In 1981 we returned to China and found the location of the old prison camp. Hank and a fellow POW, Dr. J. R. Bloomfield, had tears in their eyes as they walked through the iron gates.

In 1989, while touring Santa Barbara's sister city, a senior Japanese gentleman served as our docent guide. I asked him where he was in WWII. He told me he was captain of a gunboat on the Whangpoo River. Hank couldn't believe what he heard. From his window in the POW camp he watched the patrol boat go up and down the river. The two had much to talk about. In the course of their conversation, the old captain learned that Hank had enjoyed listening to old Japanese folk songs his guards in the POW camp played on their gramophone. When we returned home, the captain had sent a cassette of the songs to Hank. A correspondence ensued until Hank's death.

Hank Behrens and all merchant seamen had a unique history in the saga of World War II. They were forty-five years in gaining veteran status. Two years before he passed away, the government presented Hank with a military discharge and a POW medal.

ROBERT WEIL AND JIM LEVY, TWO SONS of Alabama, were best friends when the Normandy invasion was launched. Weil wrote to describe his reaction and a later visit to those beaches. He also included his friend's account of what he had gone through.

I have never had such a feeling of guilt as I had on the morning of June 6, 1944, when I awoke to learn that the invasion was on. I was a 2nd Lieutenant, still stationed stateside, but with my conscience "over there." It was some months later that I learned that my best friend landed on Omaha Beach that morning at H-Hour. He is Jim Levy, then Captain in the 81st Chemical Mortar Battalion of the 116th Infantry Regiment of the 29th Division.

Like many others, Jim never spoke to me of the invasion, and it was not until the 50th anniversary of the invasion that I read an account of it which was published on the op-ed page of the *Montgomery Advertiser*.

During the '90s, my wife and I visited Omaha Beach, the cemetery, and one end of the beach to the other. As we drove down the beach, we saw a monument on the side of the hill and drove up to see what it was. I think it was a monument dedicated to the 29th Division. There was also an American couple with two children visiting the monument.

As I stood there gazing at the profile of that long, steep hill plunging down to that beach, which appeared so narrow now, I could not imagine how our troops could land there with all the obstacles and gunfire. I said to this American chap that I didn't see how our fellows ever survived on that beach, that the Germans must have been looking right down their throats.

And the chap said, "Yes, they sure were!"

I replied, "You said that just like you were here."

"I *was* here."

"What was your division?"

"I wasn't really with a division. I was with a chemical warfare mortar battalion."

"My best friend was with a chemical mortar battalion which was supposed to land several miles up the beach, but the tide brought them down to a different point."

"The same thing happened to us. . . . Who was this friend of yours?"

"His name is Jimmy Levy."

"You don't mean Captain H. F. [Jim] Levy!"

It turned out that Jimmy was his company commander, and he was one of his platoon leaders.

This is a partial first-person account of what Jim Levy went through that day, June 6, 1944.

As we began our run for the beach, features of the terrain became gradually more distinct and flashes from our bombardment and their counter-fire grew in intensity and visibility along with the tumult of sound. The early waves of engineers had been unable to clear sufficient lanes through the obstacles (much more effective than had been intimated in training) and we were forced to move down beach, parallel to the shoreline, searching for a cleared lane to the beach.

At about this time, our LCVP [Landing Craft, Vehicle, Personnel] barely nudged a land mine, which exploded, wounding a couple of men in the bow and causing the craft to take on water alarmingly. We got another of our company's LCVPs alongside, transferred all men and weapons, but shed our packs. Another of our LCVPs was hit by artillery and a transfer of men and weapons again effected some 1,000 yards offshore with still another of B Company's LCVPs. Eventually, we located a cleared path to shore, and the craft moved as far in as possible before grounding on a sandbar. All of this time my reactions were as if I were a spectator rather than an active participant, apart from what was occurring, yet mechanically responding. It was as if the mind was overloaded with the enormity of all the external events—completely beyond our control, yet somehow functioning by rote.

The water became shoulder high on the beach side of the bar, and many men—overloaded with equipment—drowned.

We had been scheduled as the fourth wave—behind the engineers and first two waves of infantry (close-in support units) to touch shore at H Hour plus 10 minutes. Time seemed interminable and really at a standstill. Gradually, the number of men at the waterline (living, wounded, dead) increased.

Believing that it was better to be killed inland than at the water's edge, trickles of men moved up the steep face of the dune line—the leaders replaced by the next in line after being killed or disabled by anti-personnel devices. Heroism was commonplace, but there was no alternative. It is easy to be self-less when there seems to be no self. We too moved across what then seemed an expanse of beach, and up the narrow tape-marked path off the beach—at times through uncleared mine fields. We established a firing position on a shelf-like path some 20 feet below the rim of the dunes—and within 100 yards of the front line infantry. It later turned out that I was the only one of the four company commanders of the 81st who survived "D" Day.

Our position above the beach and below the top of the dune line was like a grandstand seat at a spectacle we would have preferred not to watch. We were reasonably sheltered from direct weapon fire, except the few still occupied fortifications.

By way of a personal postscript. I returned to Normandy and Omaha Beach in late September 1987 for my first and only visit. It was a tremendously emotional experience and rekindled memories and feelings long dormant. I could determine within 100 yards just where we had come ashore and set up. Faces, thoughts, sounds, and happenings came flooding back—many I did not want resurrected.

We visited the American Cemetery high on the Norman hills overlooking Omaha Beach and a more serene, appropriate, immaculate, and peaceful setting I cannot imagine. A memorial stands at the north end where you enter the cemetery. A semi-circular colonnade in an arch—above which was inscribed: "These Endured All and Gave All That Justice Among Nations Might Prevail and That Mankind Might Enjoy Freedom and Inherit Peace." In the middle distance, dividing the long avenue of lawn, stands a small circular chapel; above this was inscribed: "This Embattled Shore, Portal of Freedom, Is Forever Hallowed by the Ideals, Valor, Sacrifices of Our Fellow Countrymen." How well are these lessons learned and remembered? Standing there in appreciation, sadness, and long postponed grief, I could only wonder—"Why not me?"

AN ESTABLISHED FIGURE IN AMERICAN life is John Whitehead, a former senior partner at the Wall Street firm of Goldman Sachs and a deputy secretary of state in the administration of George Bush, who was the last of the World War II veterans to become president. Upon returning to New York following his State Department service, Whitehead became chairman of the International Rescue Committee, a private organization working tirelessly on the problems of refugees from strife around the world.

I asked him to reflect on his war years.

I've read your book with great interest. I'm not sure that those of us who served our country in World War II deserve to call ourselves the "greatest" generation. Like any group of Americans, we were a mixed bag. But I agree that we do seem to share some common differences from other generations and I know that I would not choose to switch to another generation, even if I could.

What accounts for these differences? World War II was universally accepted by all of us who participated as a "just war." There was never a question of whether or not we were on the right side.

It was a long war, too. We were in it, most of us, for a bigger part of our lives than we had expected. While we often bitched to each other about how it was interfering with whatever it was we planned to do, we never questioned that we were in it to the end. It was a war that had to be won and we would willingly stay the course.

Just as everyone remembers where they were when President Kennedy was shot, so, too, people in my generation remember where they were when the Japanese bombed Pearl Harbor. It was Sunday, December 7, 1941, at 2:00 P.M., and I was manning the checkout desk at the Haverford College library, working off the hours of one of my various work scholarships. The attack was big news and I knew my life would never be the same.

Two of my classmates, Paul Cope and Chris Cadbury, proposed that we drive down to Washington that night and hear the President declare war. It was a little silly because, of course, we had no way to get into the Capitol where the speech was to take place.

Nevertheless, off we went in Chris's ancient jalopy, and stood the next day on the Capitol steps and listened to the famous "date which will live in infamy" speech. We felt very much part of it, and so we were. It was to be a war that involved everyone.

There were a few Haverford students, it being a Quaker college, who were conscientious objectors and refused to register. Others, who registered but then declared themselves conscientious objectors, were, if they could prove a lifetime belief in pacifism, assigned to "alternative service," which meant work on a farm or driving an ambulance or some similar nonmilitary work. The boards did a pretty good job in separating the suddenly opportunistic pacifists from those with lifetime, deeply held religious beliefs. I had half a dozen Quaker classmates who fell into this category.

The rest of us were subject to be drafted at any time and most of us looked around for an alternative military program that would permit us to graduate before being called up. My friend and classmate Bob MacCrate and I discovered just such a program. It was a Navy Supply Corps program which, if we qualified, would allow us to graduate, then commission us as ensigns in the Navy, then send us for 90 days to Harvard Business School, which had been taken over for the duration by the Navy, to learn Navy accounting, and then send us off to sea.

I was called to active duty in June of 1943, assigned temporarily to the Brooklyn Navy Yard, and immediately assigned as Commanding Officer(!) of the 20th Street pier in South Brooklyn while awaiting the next class at HBS [Harvard Business School]. Here I was exposed, maybe for the first time, to being way over my head. Come to think of it, life for me has been a series of over-my-head experiences from which I had to struggle my way out.

Whitehead was assigned to the USS *Thomas Jefferson*, where he lived comfortably and relished his position as the ship's

supply officer. That often involved borrowing one of the new landing craft so he
could motor over to other ships and trade
for the supplies he needed. He quickly became a deft helmsman, and someone was
watching.

His commanding officer called him to a
private meeting in the captain's quarters.
Whitehead's account of the meeting follows.

"I want to assign you to some extra
duty," he said.

"Yes, sir."

"Ensign R. L. Jones, one of my boat
officers, has become ill and is going to
be leaving the ship, and if you're willing
and able, I'd like you to replace him
temporarily for the next several weeks."

"Yes, sir."

"I've been watching you going back
and forth to the dock. You've become
pretty good at handling an LCVP."

"Yes, sir."

Now, my normal duties on the ship
had to do with paying the crew, paying
other bills, and helping procure what-

ever supplies the ship needed to operate. My so-called battle station was up on the signal bridge, the very top of the ship, where with others I was to identify incoming airplanes as friend or foe. While these duties had their risks—enemy bombings, kamikaze planes, torpedoes, etc.—they were not exactly hand-to-hand combat.

What the Captain was asking me to do was to be a boat officer in the upcoming invasion, which meant being in charge of a group of four or five LCVPs, each carrying 20 Army or Marine infantrymen from our mother ship to an enemy beach, usually at the beginning of an invasion. This was another kettle of fish!

But what could I do? I couldn't say no. And so I said yes. The Captain stood up, shook my hand, wished me luck, and that was that. I kind of floated back to my cabin, both proud and scared. Ed Carmody was there and I told him what had just happened. I think he looked at me with new respect. I don't think he thought too much of supply officers.

As soon as we reached Portsmouth, [England,] the ship was put under tight security. In Navy lingo, the ship was "sealed." No arrivals or departures. No liberty. No mail. Lots of briefings and, for me, lots to learn. Lots of poring over maps and looking at photographs of the shoreline. Lots of clambering up into an LCVP on its davits on the deck to be sure I knew every inch of it. We were to land 2,000 soldiers from the 29th Division on Dog Red Beach in the Omaha Sector of the beaches of Normandy.

Finally, on June 4, the word came to go, in spite of the weather. It was a false alarm. The weather was too bad, and partway across the channel we were ordered to turn around and come back to Portsmouth. It was a bit of a letdown.

Twenty-four hours later, however, late in the afternoon of June 5, we left again, and this was the real thing. The slower ships went first and the fastest ships last so that we would all arrive on the beach at the same time. There were hundreds of ships. It was still stormy, raining really hard, and the sea was choppy. The crossing was uneventful. No submarines.

When we were loaded, my five LCVPs found each other, formed a circle like a cat chasing its tail, and waited for other boats to form up. It was pitch dark, drizzling, and cold and the air was dark with diesel fumes. The sea was quite choppy and within a few minutes everyone was seasick. Picture 20 men, all standing packed into a 24-foot flat-bottomed boat for four hours, heavily laden with rifles and packs, all seasick. It was pretty miserable.

It was very noisy. The sound of the engines of all the boats made it impossible to shout back and forth from boat to boat and we used walkie-talkies to communicate. Somehow our five boats kept together. By about four o'clock, the first faint light of dawn began to appear and it was easier to identify the other boats. Lost boats began to find their mates. Before long, we began to hear the deep-throated explosions of 16-inch shells fired at the beach from battleships farther out at sea. And then the drone of [planes] overhead carrying paratroopers from the 82nd and 101st Airborne Divisions to land behind the beach. It was very comforting to see that some things seemed to be working as they were supposed to.

At about 800 yards, we were released to make the final run into the beach on our own. Our five little boats were still together and seemed ready to go. It was light enough now for them to see hand signs and for me to see my watch. It was five minutes of six and I waved them on in. When we got within about 100 yards of the beach, we saw there was ahead of us a solid phalanx of steel obstacles designed to keep LCVPs from landing. We had been prepared for these obstacles, which were called Element C, but not for such a solid alignment in front of us. I signaled our boats to come to a dead stop. If we had continued on to Dog Red Beach straight ahead, we all would have been hung up on those obstacles in water too deep to debark the troops. I signaled our five boats to turn sharp left parallel to the beach. After about 100 yards we found an opening and headed for the beach again. Our boats were now a little mixed up with the boats designated to land where we were now heading, but the beach was wide enough for all of us.

It was about this time that the first German mortar shell exploded, right at the waterline of the beach that we had been heading for. But we were now about to hit the beach next door and had no time to worry about mortars. The impact of the boats hitting the ground was supposed to be enough to jar loose the boat ramps, which [would fall] forward in the water, letting the soldiers debark. It worked for everyone else but our boat. Our ramp stayed closed. I left my post in back of the coxswain and went forward to help the bowman loosen the ramp. After a few blows from the hammer, our ramp came down too, and our soldiers debarked. I glanced at the other boats in our wave and saw that they were ready to withdraw.

Our job now was to get off the beach as quickly as possible to get out of the way of the second wave, which was to land directly behind us. We raised our ramps and retreated without any serious problems.

We also realized that our job with the soldiers we had landed was completed, but that theirs was only beginning, and that they had days and weeks and months ahead before their job was over. In the meantime, we were returning to the *Jefferson* for a good hot shower and a hot brunch served for the officers in the wardroom. Rather incongruous for a group of men who had just landed on the first wave at Normandy. The soldiers were the real heroes.

There was one moment of D-Day which, rather strangely, remains more vivid in my mind than anything else. It was a quiet moment, a moment of peace and introspection after a very long day of noise and fear, of chaos and seasickness, of little acts of courage, and of death.

It was about 3:00 and we had made our second landing of the day and would soon be starting again the two-hour trip back to the *T.J.* The beach was now secure. My five little boats had all made it in without serious problems and we were actually a little ahead of schedule. The ship's crew had only had two casualties from the landing. The Army lieutenant from my boat was now busy trying to get ashore a large machine gun and, for the first time since 2:00 A.M., I had a free moment.

I clambered off the boat—we were stuck on a little shoal in about two feet of water—and walked a few yards up the beach. I took a few deep breaths and looked around me. The dead and wounded had been moved up to the first dune and were being cared for.

Equipment—guns and food and ammunition—was being unloaded, along with more troops. As far as I could see, in both directions, LCVPs were landing, unloading, and withdrawing and I realized that what I could see was less than 5% of the landing beaches. It wasn't orderly, but it wasn't chaos either. I got the sense that it was going to work, that what had looked like such a disaster only a few hours earlier was beginning to look like it had a chance.

I felt thankful, of course, that I seemed to have survived the worst part. I took a few deep breaths and felt suddenly elated, proud to be having even a tiny part in what was maybe the biggest battle of all history. At that moment, soaked to the skin, seasick, dead tired, cold, still scared, I would not have wanted to be anywhere else.

A NUMBER OF VETERANS WROTE poignant accounts of their fear during combat. One of them, Frank Hancock of Madison, Alabama, told a touching story of a comrade who made a difficult decision as the 399th Infantry, 100th Division, crossing northern Europe, battled German forces in the Vosges Mountains. He begins with an episode from his memoir, "An Improbable Machine Gunner."

This day is a little quieter. We listen for the distant cough of the mortars and move back in the dugout to escape shrapnel when the rounds hit the trees overhead. We know the sounds: our 105-mm artillery and 60- or 81-mm mortars; their 88-mm cannon and 50- or 80-mm mortars. The ratio seems to hold; about 15 to 20 rounds go out for each one coming in. Firing continues all day. Some of our rounds fall short; a 105-mm shell hits the edge of our dugout; I am sitting inside when it bursts, not more than 2 feet from my head. My ears ring from the concussion, but the frozen dirt and logs stopped all of the fragments.

We hang a blanket to separate the dugout from the opening by the gun.

Now there are three of us; one hour on and two off. Not bad! But the two sleepers are so crowded that they must turn over at the same time!

I am roused from sleep by the man I am to relieve; he lights a candle while I bundle up and put on my pistol belt. I crawl over to the hanging blanket and whisper: "Put the candle out!" He shields it with his hand and I slip under the blanket. A light blinks over my shoulder.

Furious because I think the light came from the candle, I move quickly behind the gun, and my foot strikes something in the bottom of the hole. I pick it up; it feels like a metal goose egg with a raised seam around it. I hold it inside the blanket. "What the hell is this? *It's a Kraut grenade! Git it out of here!*" I turn and throw the grenade, blind, in the dark, remembering where there is a gap in the trees. Nothing happens.

"Where is he?" The woods are silent. Nothing stirs while I strain my eyes and ears. All night I ponder: "How could he

have gotten so close? What would have happened if it had not been a dud? Why did my buddy take time to insert 'the hell' in the middle of his warning?" The half-second might have been fatal if the grenade fuse had been alive.

The next evening near dusk I venture out again, and peer out from behind the tree above the dugout. With the binoculars I see a column of Germans lined up at what looks to be a horse-drawn mess cart. I pick out a tree which marks their location and then scramble down behind the gun and sight it on the tree.

A twig snaps behind me and I whirl with drawn pistol; it is our old Company Commander, now acting as Battalion Commander. I give him the binoculars and show him where the Germans are still busy dishing chow. I tell him about where the gun is sighted. He looks, then hands me the binoculars and says, "Well, what are you waiting for?"

I crouch behind the gun and fire about half a belt, maybe a hundred rounds, while traversing the gun around the tree landmark. Then I look back to where the Captain had been standing, and the forest is quite empty. I duck back into the dugout as mortar shells burst in the tree above us.

The other gunner asks: "What was that all about?" And when I tell him, he thinks it is pretty funny that the Captain vanished so quickly. It is the first, but not the last time that I see Captain Derryberry at the front.

That night I return from the chow jeep to find a new neighbor. During my absence of a half-hour or less, a rifleman has killed a German soldier, not 20 yards away from our gun. In the commotion of men going to eat, the gunner did not see the German approaching our hole, but a rifleman did. I wonder if [the dead German] is the same man who dropped the grenade in our hole the night before.

Trees move in the wind and their moonlight shadows shift across the figure lying still in the snow, so that he appears to move. I know that he is quite dead, for the medic checked him. We will not jeopardize a recovery team to bring a fallen foe from this exposed position. He will keep well enough in the bitter cold.

A few days in reserve are like heaven, walking in the streets of Siersthal, [France,] getting showers and clean clothes, three hot meals, and sleeping indoors, warm and dry. After a night or two of sleeping inside, my hips and shoulders get sore from sleeping on the floor. In the dugouts we smooth little depressions in the ground and we are padded with winter clothing.

Late afternoon, we pack to return to the front that night after dark. I show the squad how to put a new barrel in the machine gun. The old barrel looks pretty good, but someone has decided to replace it; maybe because it sat out in the woods for weeks without being oiled every day. Then too, it was not cleaned after Lt. Witt and I had fired a total of several hundred rounds through it. And I have no idea how much this gun has been used in the last two months!

The new gun barrel is full of Cosmoline, a black preservative. More like asphalt than grease; it is hard when cold. I warm the barrel next to the stove and finally get a ramrod to carry a cleaning patch through to the chamber.

Smitty the ammo bearer watches me install the barrel, and moves close to my side. At 27 he is the oldest man in the squad, maybe the oldest in the platoon. A recent draftee, he is good-humored, and well liked. Quietly, he says: "Frank, I'm not going back with you." Amazed, I put down the gun barrel. "What?" This is unheard of—what will they do to him?

"I'm not going back. I've got two little girls at home, and I want to live to see them again. I want to get back to them with enough of me left to be able to take care of them." He shows me their picture. Little charmers!

I like how lucky I am still to be single; the thought of leaving a family; or worse, coming home crippled, to be a burden—but I say: "I can't do anything about it, you'd better talk to the Lieutenant."

I install the packing around the gun barrel and fill the jacket with antifreeze: "GI" Prestone, in OD-painted cans. My mind follows the ammo bearer; men have been shot for less! We miss him later that night when we move out to relieve another battalion on the front.

I need not have worried; our understanding Company Commander assigns him to permanent KP for the rest of the war. Our kitchen is seldom out of artillery range, but it is almost never hit and has few—or no—casualties. He also serves . . . and what he did that day was an act of courage and love.

In the middle of the night, carrying our guns and bedrolls to the front, we are almost to our new positions when we pass a dead white horse and shell-splintered trees.

I think of the options: of going home proud of my service; in shame as a deserter; or more likely, disabled or not at all.

The kitchen seems a good place to be.

GEORGE WELLS HOLDS THE RECORD, with his friend and fellow pilot Fred Dyer, for the greatest number of bombing missions flown by a U.S. soldier during World War II. By the time he was twenty-six, his life had taken some dramatic turns.

I was born in 1919 and raised out in the country in southern New Jersey. Our family was doing all right finally, for country folks prior to the Depression. I graduated from Haddon Heights High School as president of the senior class in 1937. My parents couldn't afford to send me to college, but I was able to get a job as an apprentice in a print shop for $8.00 a week. Through the small local bank, I arranged to buy a secondhand car for $100.00. The bank let me pay $2.00 a week and no money down. I paid my parents $4.00 a week for room and board which left $2.00 a week for gas and other expenses, but not enough to take a date to a movie.

After I'd been working for two years at the print shop, in 1939, union organizers came in and told me my salary would be $16.00 a week if the print shop employees voted to join the union. Of course, we voted for it, but the print shop in order to be able to pay the increased wages laid off the last two persons hired, one of which was me.

My brother, Oliver, ten years older, had gone to college and had friends in the National Guard. He told me he was sure our country was going to be in a war and I should join the National Guard immediately and apply to take a course called the "Ten Series." When completed, it would qualify me to become a 2nd Lieutenant in the National Guard. This course usually took a working person about two years to complete. Being out of work, I completed the course in six months and passed it.

Right after Pearl Harbor, the Army Air Corps needed many more pilot officers due to their great expansion and solicited young ground force officers to transfer to the Army Air Corps for pilot training. I thought it was a great challenge and applied for it. I was promoted to 1st Lieutenant in the Field Artillery. Then I was transferred to the Army Air Corps for pilot training in 1942. I completed all the training and became the "First Pilot" on a B-25 crew in the famous Mitchell Bomber.

In 1943, my crew and I were sent overseas and joined the famous 340th B-25 Bomb Group, one of three bomb groups in the 47th Bomb Wing.

The 340th became known as the "Bridge Busters" for our many pinpoint attacks destroying bridges. Many bombing records were made by our unit. One of the most notable was when Major Fred Dyer and I established the record for the highest number of bomber missions flown by any U.S. pilot in World War II in one continuous overseas tour. We each flew 102 missions without returning home to the U.S. for rest. After a lot of effort, we were allowed to fly our 100th mission together in the same plane, which was also flying its 100th mission. We flipped a coin to see who would fly as first pilot on the mission. I won the toss and flew as first pilot and Dyer was co-pilot and formation commander for the mission. This was covered by the media.

We had thought this 100th mission was the record for World War II; but the media, who were there for the event, advised us someone had flown 50 missions in one tour in the Pacific theater and 51 missions in the European theater, during two separate overseas tours. So, Dyer and I got permission to fly two more missions and jointly share the record for the most missions in one continuous tour for any U.S. pilot in World War II.

One specific fact that I believe is God related is that I never felt very much apprehension in all of my combat experiences. I do not really understand it. I had confidence that I could meet

challenges and this was a great blessing
because many had great fear. It was also
an advantage to be the pilot because to
some degree I had more control than
the others, like the gunners, bombardiers, etc.

My original bombardier, "Red" Reichard, was totally frightened of combat.
Whenever he was assigned for the next
day, he couldn't sleep; he perspired,
rolled, and tossed all night, as he was
convinced he would not survive the
war. However, it did not affect his tal-
ent at all, and in spite of great anxiety
he became one of the lead bombardiers
for the group. In our particular group,
we did not maintain crew integrity, and
he and I only flew together a few times
in combat.

It is amazing that our two philoso-
phies came to play within seconds of
each other. On a bombing mission over
Anzio beachhead, Red Reichard was
the lead bombardier in the first flight
over the target. I was the lead pilot of
the second flight over the target; sepa-

ration between the two planes was about 50 yards.

His plane was hit with an 88-millimeter anti-aircraft shell. The plane exploded and all were killed. Within two or three seconds, an 88-millimeter shell went right through one side of my plane's tail section and out the other side. It did not explode! Each of those shells contained a time fuse, as well as a contact fuse on the nose section, which is supposed to explode on contact. His plane exploded. My plane had nothing more than two holes about six inches across in the tail section. There was no other damage to the plane and it was completely flyable.

Another bombardier of note in our squadron was Joe Heller, who later became famous when he wrote *Catch-22*. Many years later, when I read the book, I saw myself as Capt. Wren, who flew all the time. Heller wrote Captain Wren "enjoyed flying combat missions and begged nothing more of life and Colonel Cathcart than the opportunity to continue flying them. They had flown hundreds of combat missions and wanted to fly hundreds more." . . .

I received the Silver Star, two Distinguished Flying Crosses, the Air Medal with 12 oak-leaf clusters, Joint Service Commendation Medal, European African–Middle Eastern Campaign Medal with 7 battle stars, World War II Victory Medal, A.F. Longevity Service Award with one silver oak-leaf cluster, and the National Defense Service Medal with one bronze star.

I contacted Joseph Heller and asked if he remembered Captain Wells.

I remember him very well . . . but [Captain Wren] is not him. It's based on someone who had his position, which was the operations officer. I think that the one similarity to him in the book is this: George Wells just flew missions endlessly and without fear, and I just put that into *Catch-22* . . . it struck me as kind of heroic and . . . unreal.

He (Wells) doesn't know me or re-member me because I was a replace-ment for one of fifty or seventy. I doubt we had any conversations. He was one of those people I looked up to—I was only nineteen or twenty years old, and joining a combat group! They had been around the world in combat, and I joined up only in Corsica. I was a kid and these were people I looked up to.

IN *THE GREATEST GENERATION* I WROTE about the men of the 8th Air Force, which conducted the long, dangerous bombing runs from England over Europe. I had no complaints from the pilots and crews as-signed to the 15th Air Force, in southern Eu-rope, but I did get a terrifying account of a first mission from Robert Dyas of the 15th Air Force, who went on to fly fifty-two mis-sions in the cockpits of B-24s. He sent along passages from his yet-to-be-published book, "The Liberators."

It sounded as if we were flying through a heavy hail storm. Some of the spent flak was penetrating our ship's thin aluminum skin. Bomb-bay doors were again opened, the lead ship in our "box" dropped by "Pathfinder," and [each of] the remaining ships in our box then "toggled off his drop." Our bombardier yelled "Bombs away!" over the intercom, and what was left of the original formation went into a steep, left-turning dive toward the ground. We were still in the air and still flyable. Flak had penetrated most of the ship, hydraulic fluid was spewed all over the deck as several hydraulic lines had been punctured, spent 50mm shells were piled high at all the gunners' positions, and one of the crew members could be seen, still shooting continuously out of his waist-gun position. Another crew member, with his hands clamped over his earphones as if to shut out the noise, was quivering as if he had the jungle plague, but still kept on firing. No blood yet, and no one physically hurt, thanks be to whoever is up there looking out for us.

Suddenly, directly out of the sun and coming straight at us was a single ME-109 with all guns blazing. Our nose gunner was blasting away with his trigger on "continuous fire" but our top turret gun was silent, and he should have been shooting at that crazy Hun as he was probably directly in his crosshairs. The warning light for fire in the number two engine was flashing rapidly and our engine instruments told us number two was "cooked" (inoperable and with fire). The Captain ordered that I "feather" number two and push the fire extinguisher button for that engine, which I did immediately. While we continued to try and get back into our formation, we found that this was impossible due to the decrease in power caused by the dead engine. As our airspeed and altitude slowly diminished, we found ourselves a sitting duck for the Nazi fighters still attacking us from all directions.

Our gunners were firing continuously from all gun positions, except for the top turret, as we were being raked by machine-gun fire from the Hun.

The Hun fighters, which had been dogging us all the way and which had been kept at bay by the accuracy of our gunners, abruptly disappeared. Far in the distance we could see the American fighters coming out of the south. They caught up with the slowly retreating Nazi aircraft just as we were approaching the lofty peaks of the Alps. Suddenly, an American P-38 "Lightning" peeled off his chase after a ME-109 that he was about to shoot down, when he noticed our crippled B-24. Without a second thought for his very possible air victory, he pulled alongside us and pointed to his radio headset trying to have us obtain radio contact. Captain Jawatte shook his head, indicating that we could not respond. Jawatte pointed ahead, trying to explain what he was going to try to attempt. The pilot of the P-38 threw up both of his hands to gesture that he understood and, shoving his throttle ahead, flew around us. He then took up a position directly in front of us, matched our airspeed, and guided us through the treacherous mountain range. The P-38 had more sophisticated radar and sonar equipment aboard than a B-24 and he was better able to judge how far away those jagged and deadly peaks were. If it were not for the P-38's courageous pilot leading us through the small openings in the Alps, I am sure we would have crashed into the side of the mountains. Truly, a brave, brave man! Sacrificing a certain kill in downing a German plane, he risked his life to guide us through the Alps.

Finally, after what seemed like an eternity, we broke free of the pinnacles and saw green grass and valleys below. The P-38 dropped back, and with a wave of his hand and a flip of his wings, turned back to rejoin the action.

The pilot [Captain Jawatte] suggested that I go aft to check out the extent of the damage and try to find out what happened to our top turret gunner. I could not believe the damage suffered by the B-24. How it stayed in the air was a major miracle. The bomb-bay doors were closed but were riddled with so many flak and machine-gun bullet holes, they looked like Swiss cheese. There were so many large holes and openings, I had no trouble seeing the ground below. How any of our gunners survived was a phenomenon. No one could possibly have survived in the twisted metal and plastic covering the entire rear end of our Liberator. There was hydraulic fluid, smelly and covering the entire deck. The waist guns were still hot to the touch and the smell of cordite was overpowering. Spent 50mm shell casings covered the entire floor and you had to be damn careful as you picked your way through. The tail gunner and the ball turret gunner were just emerging from their coops and they looked like something out of a Frankenstein movie. Faces blackened, eyes popping out of their sockets, hands quivering, not saying a single word.

Also emerging from the farthest reaches of the ship's rear end was our presumably lost original top turret gunner. What a spectacle he was! Still wearing his full flying regalia, including his oxygen mask and a carry-along oxygen bottle, he had three hard-to-come-by flak vests strapped around his entire body. He was shaking so badly I was afraid that he would fall. No one said a word to him and he did not speak.

On the ground below, we noted several ambulances and fire trucks assembled in our landing area. As we all held our collective breaths, I think everyone aboard gave a silent prayer.

Our fears were ungrounded as Jawatte greased that big wounded bird in as if it had eyes of its own.

With mission number one under my belt, I felt I was invincible.

ONE OF THE MOST ASTONISHING WAR stories I received actually begins in Poland. It came to me from Dr. Zdzislaw Wesolowski, a college professor in Miami. It's his description of the life of his father, Stefan P. Wesolowski.

My father's military service in the Polish armed forces started in 1918 when as a boy of nine he volunteered to serve in the liberation of Lwów. His heroic action resulted in his being awarded the highest Polish decoration for valor, the Order of the Virtuti Militari, which is equal in stature to our American Medal of Honor. By 1921 he was a seasoned war veteran and at the age of twelve participated in the Third Silesian Uprising, during which time he was wounded, decorated with the Cross of Valor, and promoted to the rank of corporal, becoming the youngest noncommissioned officer in the history of the Polish armed forces.

After his war services in the liberation of Poland, my father joined the newly forming Polish merchant marine as a cabin boy on one of the first ships of that fleet, the *Gazolina*. . . . On the instruction of the captain he sewed a Polish flag. In a short ceremony he raised the flag as an act of commissioning the ship into the Polish merchant marine, which had been absent from the Baltic Sea for 350 years. And so he became Poland's first sailor of the fleet.

In 1922, Poland was reorganizing the Polish armed forces and a call was made by Marshal Jozef Piludski, the commander in chief, to all veterans to join the armed forces. My father answered that call, presenting his military papers and decorations to the Polish Navy. At the age of 13 he was enrolled in the Polish Navy with the rank of petty officer and placed in charge of a ten-man naval observation post in Gdynia. This unprecedented event did not deter him from carrying out his duties even though his subordinates were twice his age.

Because of his twenty years of federal service, Father was thinking of retiring in 1938 and with my mother was looking for a retirement location. Little did they know that Adolf Hitler had other plans for the Polish people. By the end of August of 1938, Father received orders to report for active duty aboard the Polish destroyer the ORP *Blyskawica,* as a signalist. Father never returned to Poland and took part in the Battles of Narvik and the Atlantic. Being wounded several times and declared unfit for military duty in 1941, he now joined the Polish merchant marine as an officer. His bravery and professional reputation became well known and in 1943 while his ship was in the Brooklyn Naval Shipyard, Father was invited to meet with the commander of the U.S. Army Transportation Corps. The commander offered him the position of 2nd officer aboard an auxiliary aircraft carrier, the USAT *Ganandoc,* which was being refitted for convoy duty. At that time Father was still a citizen of Poland.

Father accepted the position at once, because he believed that by serving with the American forces he could do more to help Poland. After several convoys, the captain became ill and Father took over the command of the *Ganandoc*. The *Ganandoc* took part in the invasion of Normandy and was damaged to such an extent that Father was instructed to scuttle the ship. Instead he and his crew worked fearlessly and returned the ship to Southampton for repairs. Needless to say, the whole ship and Father were decorated. While the *Ganandoc* was being repaired, Father was given command of a large seagoing tug, the USALT 533, which took part in convoy duty and salvage operations. On one occasion, the ship sailed into a minefield. Father took immediate action and warned the convoy commander to reroute the convoy. By doing so, Father saved the whole invasion fleet from considerable loss of life and equipment. For his heroics, he was later decorated with the Bronze Star for Valor. After the war, he joined the U.S. merchant marine and sailed worldwide until his final retirement in Miami Beach.

While Father was with the Polish and American fleet, my mother, my brother, and I were in German-occupied Poland, living in constant fear, deprivation, and danger. When the war started, I remember Mother carrying my younger brother Jeremii with me running after her across battlefields for safety while being shot at by both sides. During the years 1939–1946 my mother took care of us as well as she could by begging for food and working as slave labor in German barracks and hospitals. We moved constantly across Poland, out of harm's way. One day the Gestapo surrounded our hut and arrested Mother. They held her for interrogation for days because she had received a letter from Father via Switzerland, which was rerouted by a friend from London. It was a miracle that she was later released.

When the war ended in 1945, Father left no stone unturned looking for us, and with the help of the U.S. Embassy in Warsaw was able to locate us, being informed that we survived the war. In March of 1946 Father landed at Warsaw airport in the uniform of an American naval officer with secret orders signed by General Eisenhower. We were informed several weeks in advance of his possible arrival and left Gdynia for Warsaw. I still remember that fantastic day when I saw my father return. I was playing in the ruins of Warsaw. The joy was overwhelming. His return to Poland to get us out of Communist Soviet-occupied Poland was another one of his acts of bravery. He could have been arrested and shot because he was still a Polish citizen and because he served with the Americans. Father arranged for our departure from Poland and on July 20th, 1946, our ship, the SS *Washington,* a troop carrier, passed by the Statue of Liberty.

To try my father's life at sea, I joined the U.S. merchant marine for a few years during the Korean War, but later decided to enlist in the U.S. Air Force, retiring with the rank of captain in the reserves. Now I serve in the reserves as a colonel in the South Carolina State Guard. After receiving my higher education, I became a college administrator and currently serve as a professor at Florida Memorial College in Miami. My brother, Jeremii, also obtained a doctoral degree and held high-ranking executive positions in the pharmaceutical industry, retiring in Yorba Linda, California.

This short letter does not do justice to our parents, who dedicated their lives to two nations, their family, and the community. My parents gave us support and care and examples to live by. They sacrificed their own well-being to help my brother and me to complete our education. My father passed to me a thousand-year Polish tradition of military virtue . . . he believed that service in the military was the highest possible contribution one can make to the nation he truly loves. He loved democracy and freedom as exemplified by his contributions to Poland and the United

States. He never neglected his responsibility as a father and husband. His love and commitment to his wife and sons was total and complete, as is my love to my wife, Emilia, and our children, Juliana, Stefan, and Wanda. My brother, Jeremii, shares my views in his commitment to his wife, Alicia, and their children, Ashley, Andrea, Alexa, and Jeremii, Jr.

Our mother, Antonina, was a unique person with all the virtues of a loving and caring Polish mother even at the risk of her own life. While Father was at sea, earning a living, she cared for us and helped in our education and provided a home environment in which we found happiness. Her cooking was out of this world. When I look back to those war years I thank God and my mother for our survival. Fifteen million Poles never lived to see V-E Day.

NOT ALL WAR STORIES ARE ABOUT combat, heroism, life and death. Raymond

Daum described his final, never-to-be-forgotten days as a combat photographer, and the rescue of priceless artifacts from the personal collection of Ludwig van Beethoven:

I was 19 in 1942, when I enlisted in the U.S. Army Signal Corps. I served in the Army as a motion picture combat cameraman following a semester's study at the University of Southern California's Department of Cinema. I was armed with a .45 revolver, and it was my job to "shoot the shooters" with a government-issue 12-pound 35mm Eyemo movie camera. We were assigned to fighting units in the European Theater of Operations, mainly the ground forces of infantry divisions. In one armored attack at about the time of the Battle of the Bulge, I was wounded as 300 German prisoners of war were rounded up at the end of a long tank battle. I got in the way of German artillery as I walked alongside our Sherman tanks and was whacked by an 88 shell that pierced my helmet as I knelt to reload my camera.

I returned to combat two days later, along with scores of GIs also hit in that German barrage. There is nothing like a close call on a battlefield to make the morning more beautiful, to make the green fields more fragrant, and to make life seem like a worthwhile journey.

There are so many experiences that your book has awakened in me—so many memories good, and some not so good. The time a Graves Registration Unit GI called me over as he processed identification of dead German soldiers lying in the fields after a firefight. He handed me a small photograph from the wallet of one young soldier. It was a picture of Ginger Rogers! (Who was my favorite movie star, too.)

As the Allied armies had penetrated deeper into Germany, and the German High Command could see that the end of the war was near, Field Marshal Hermann Göring, Commander of the German Luftwaffe, who was infamous for his looting of Europe's artistic treasures, dispatched orders to all [German] museums to disperse their collections so that they would not be looted and pillaged by the invading armies. One of these historical sites was the Beethoven-Haus in Bonn. This was the birthplace—the home—of the composer and had been converted into a museum. It was known that the museum collection included three pianos owned by Beethoven, several musical instruments, and oil portraits important to him in his life—including Joseph Haydn, Mozart, Schubert, and others. Just months before, German transport trucks had appeared at the museum, where the treasures were quickly loaded and the convoy, headed by Dr. Wildemann [the museum's curator], travelled to various rural sites in the Rhineland Province.

We took back roads. It would be a long journey to avoid the major highways that were littered with destroyed tanks and abandoned equipment left by the Germans. And what we dreaded most were the land mines put in place by the retreating enemy. I thought to myself that if this journey had taken place only a few days earlier we might have taken enemy fire. As we drove through small villages, it was obvious that some Germans were afraid to come out of their houses. They were not sure the war had ended, but some villages had white cloths of surrender hanging from windows or on poles. The children were the bravest, coming out of their homes into the street pointing handmade toy guns at us, for most of the populace in these rural regions refused to believe their country had actually capitulated. I caught the scenes in my camera's viewfinder as we approached each site on Wildemann's list [of hiding places for the museum's treasures]. I would jump out of the truck's cab as doors were hesitantly opened and I could see faces of fear—the occupants not sure what fate awaited them until Wildemann smiled reassuringly, speaking quickly, as my camera whirred harmlessly. Then out they would come—the crates, the trunks, and, from Homburg Castle, the three pianos that had been hidden in the castle's dungeon. Finally, we were led to the Siegen salt mines, where the precious art works and boxes of musical manuscripts had been stored, because the salt deposits absorbed the moisture from the air, leaving temperatures and humidity virtually constant.

Now, at the end of our quest, Dr. Wildemann asked me to hand-carry a huge bundle of autographed music manuscripts—the originals and so priceless! The manuscripts for the piano sonatas were present—including the "Moonlight Sonata," and scores of the Pastoral and Ninth Symphonies!

We finally reached Bonn, which was like a ghost town with blocks and blocks of incendiary ruins. Dr. Wildemann signaled for us to turn down a street with a sign which read, "Beethoven-Haus Gasse" (Beethoven House Street). We came to a stop before a large boarded-up portal. The first thing I noticed were German words, EINTRITT VERBOTEN — MUSEUM! ("Entry Forbidden—Museum"). In filming inside and outside the museum, I was shown, by the caretaker, the room upstairs where Beethoven was born in 1770. One question we all asked ourselves which had to be answered: How was it possible that this little two-hundred-year-old tinderbox building had survived the severe and prolonged incendiary bombings? The German caretaker's story was one of the most amazing to come out of the war. Each night, he told us—translated by Dr. Wildemann—that as the incendiary bombs began to fall, he would crawl up to the roof of the house with a garden hose turned on with as much pressure as it would afford, and he would spray—douse the walls and roof all night long until the bombing ceased, to keep the wood and plaster as wet as possible, for the structure to survive another night.

What a day it had been! A unique and gratifying experience for us all, and in a way I felt I had contributed somehow to the making of peace in Europe. I guess it has to be my best remembered story, and one not about the fighting, but about the mutual respect for one of mankind's most admirable accomplishments—great music.

As I look back to that day in Bonn—it had provided a moment of sanity in the hectic demise of the Third Reich. The experience proved that the only glory of war is in the hope of cooperation between the enemies afterward. At Beethoven-Haus, conquerors and the conquered had joined hands to preserve mankind's priceless heritage and culture.

VERONICA MACKEY HULICK, OF FORT Pierce, Florida, became a Navy WAVE during World War II and before long found herself assigned to a secret project. At first she didn't know what she was working on but later she discovered it was a critical part of the Allied success.

I was 20 years old when I joined the Navy WAVES [Women Accepted for Volunteer Emergency Service] in Jan. 1943. After boot camp I was sent, with a contingent, to Dayton, Ohio. We were assigned to a building across from the National Cash Register Co. We sat at a long table with a soldering iron, long threads of solder and inch-long wires of red, yellow, green, and blue. We were given a small wheel and a graph to follow. We soldered the little wires inside the wheel according to the graph. The wheel was then covered with graphite. Plastics had not been invented as yet.

I decided that I must not have passed the aptitude tests. This had to be the dumbest job in the Navy. However, I was surrounded by many bright young women, many of whom, like me, were former telephone operators.

One day my mother called to say a Navy officer was going all around my hometown, Wilmington, Delaware, asking questions about me. He went to my teachers, friends, employers, and neighbors. I didn't know what was going on, but I began to feel important.

We worked the swing shift and had one day off a week. The third week, we got 2 days off. It took 3 months to get a Sat. and Sun. off. We were constantly monitored by WAVE officers and had many sessions on security about our work.

This went on from April till October. I went on duty one day and saw something huge on a flatcar near our building. It was covered with a gray shroud. I said to myself, "I wonder what that is?" I know now it was the housing for the computer that was being built. NCR built the housing, the switches, and the wiring, and we women wired the rotor wheels.

That day we were told we were being transferred to Washington, D.C. We were assigned to barracks across the street from the Naval Communications

Annex at Nebraska and Massachusetts Avenues.

When we went on duty, we had to show our picture and number I.D. to 2 armed Marines at the gates and a Navy man at our building. The first day on duty, we were taken into a chapel and a Navy officer stood in the pulpit and told us if we talked about what we were working on at this station, we would be shot! About 500 women ran these 120 computers on a shift. It was constant for the next 2½ years. We never breached security, we'd gotten the message loud and clear.

The computer was nicknamed "the Bombe" because of the noise it made while running. The word "computer" was not in the vocabulary at that time. Also missing in those times was air-conditioning. The oppressive heat of the D.C. summers was unbelievable, but we were young and full of patriotism. We lived in two-story barracks, 50 girls on each floor. We had a bunk, a locker, and community showers. We all got along, worked hard, and had fun on our days off.

When we got a print-out from the computer we couldn't read it. We tore it off quickly, ran to a door at the end of the room, knocked, and a hand came out and took it, I presume, to a decoding room. We had 120 computers, and when we revved them up, we got a trillion combinations. Hitler once sent a message to a general. We intercepted and broke it before it reached the general's hands.

It still boggles my mind, in retrospect, that first we helped to build this computer and then ran it.

We were paid $50.00 a month for a long time because the Navy did not know what to call us. We weren't radiomen or yeomen. Finally, after a year and a half we were given a new rating, a "Q," and raised to $60.00 a month.

When the war was over, and we were being discharged, we were taken individually into an office and told to put one hand on the Bible and take an oath that we would never talk about our work. We had a form for future employers stating they were not to ask us about our activities during World War II. Five hundred women went home, got on with their lives, and never said a word.

In 1977, President Carter declassified a lot of WWII material, and a couple of books were written about "the Bombe." The Navy never informed any of these women that the oath was lifted. My parents died never knowing what I did in the service.

In 1994 a reunion was held in Dayton, Ohio. About 80 women showed up. A Navy historian spoke to us and told us we were responsible for the sinking of between 750 and 800 German U-boats, that we shortened the war by one and possibly two years, and had saved countless lives. It was a wonderful moment. It was great to be able to tell my children and grandchildren of my work during WWII, but I wept for those who had passed away and never revealed their contribution to the war effort.

You are right, it was a different time in our history. We were patriotic, disciplined, caring, and just so thrilled to know we were doing something special to help end the war. We never sought recognition. I always thought of us as the unsung heroines of WWII.

WEIKA KOENRAAD, OF DAHLONEGA, Georgia, was a little girl in Holland during the war, and has vivid memories of the American soldiers who liberated her town in 1945. She's now an American citizen.

I was just a little girl during the Second World War, born in Haarlem, Holland, in 1937. My husband [was born] in Amsterdam [in] 1933.

The Netherlands was occupied by the Germans in 1940, and in the western part (Holland) where I lived, the liberation came only in 1945.

The scariest thought in my mind were soldiers, with black shiny boots and a gun; nobody ever smiled, there was nothing to smile about. The games we played as children were war games. We had built a play hospital and I was the nurse. My friends were wounded and brought to the hospital. There were no toys.

The most severe winter in decades was the winter in 1944. The southern part of the Netherlands was already free, but the western part which is above the river Rhine was still occupied. Because of the weather, there was nothing more to eat. Everybody was hungry and our daily meal consisted of sugar beets, which we now feed to the hogs, and tulip bulbs. I still remember the taste of tulip bulbs. It was a nice sweet taste.

Suddenly there was spring, the bad weather was gone, and it was May 1945. Big tanks rolled through the streets and for the very first time I saw people who smiled and waved to us. They were soldiers! It was like a miracle—they were supposed to be scary, and now they were friendly and smiled. They threw

Hershey's chocolate bars and chewing gum into the crowd. Something we had never seen or tasted before. I was lucky enough to catch a piece of gum. This was called by us the everlasting candy; you could chew it and it never ended. This piece of gum was, of course, shared with your friends. They all wanted to try it, but it ended up in your own mouth again.

My husband and I and our two children emigrated to the U.S.A. 22 years ago and became Americans after 5 years.

Every time I meet somebody who has served in the Second World War I give him a hug and say, "Thanks to you we are alive."

THE FATHER OF WILFRED CHATIGNY OF Amesbury, Massachusetts, served as a staff sergeant on the front lines in Germany, where he was seriously injured. He later defied the predictions of doctors who told him that he would never walk again. Following a long recuperation after the war, Wilfred Chatigny, Sr., went to work for a silversmith.

According to his son, he is intensely patriotic and humble about his contributions to
the war effort.

Dad entered France through Omaha
Beach as a Staff Sergeant in the 89th
Division in March of 1945, and spent
one week at Camp Lucky Strike. Then
his company was moved up to the front
lines. The fiercest battle they incurred
was at Koblenz, Germany, where they
crossed the Rhine and had to hold the
bridge. Shortly thereafter, they passed a
concentration camp that had been liberated by another company. Dad won't
talk about it. The only comment he
made was that it was apparent the Germans had run over all the prisoners
with their half-tracks.

Less than two months after entering
the war, Dad was shot. His company
was clearing the town of Darmstadt.
They started early one morning and Dad
said they didn't get 100 feet into town
when he got hit. The bullet entered his
thigh and exited below his stomach. He
had substantial internal injuries that

have bothered him all his life. The doctors told him he would never walk again, but he did, and still does. He credits the fact that he was always in great shape, first as an athlete in school, and then in the service after graduation in 1941. The one story Dad has told a number of times, and always gets a laugh with, is that when he woke up in the hospital two days later he couldn't understand a word anyone was saying. He asked the nurse what all the gibberish was and why he couldn't understand. Well, he was in the German ward. When he was shot, he was carrying a German Luger and a German flag. Souvenirs! They thought he was a German infiltrator, which apparently had been a problem in the field. After some discussion and a few World Series questions, Dad was moved to the American ward. He never got his souvenirs back.

VAN PARKER OF CARMICHAEL, CALIFORnia, was a veteran B-29 pilot when the war ended. He shared with us a letter he wrote to his parents about his final mission. It is part of his memoir called "Dear Folks."

Dear Folks,

Yesterday I experienced a privilege which will long live in my memory. It was my honor to lead a B-29 squadron over the Tokyo area while Japan's final surrender was in progress.

The purpose of our visit to the Japanese empire was to take part in the greatest display of aerial force ever assembled—this for the benefit of the Japanese people. What a sight! There were seemingly thousands of our airplanes in the air. Everywhere you looked you could see large formations of aircraft. The display must have struck awe and terror into the hearts of all Japanese who witnessed the spectacle.

We gave them a never-to-be-forgotten show of the aerial might which brought them to their knees.

As we flew low over Tokyo Bay and

our big battlewagon *Missouri,* where
the Japanese were signing the historic
peace documents which officially
ended this world's bloodiest conflict, I
couldn't help but feel proud that I had
played a small part in our victory.

Stretched before our eyes, and
crowding Tokyo Bay to its very shores,
were hundreds of ships. Never before
had I seen such an accumulation of
naval strength—and all ours. The Army
and Navy were everywhere.

Following bomber formation break-
up, prior to departure for home base,
our crew seized the opportunity to do
some personal reconnoitering over the
Japanese homeland; [we were] especially curious about Tokyo and its envi-
rons.

It was the first time I had flown over
Tokyo without being shot up. Because
we were flying very low and because
there were no guns firing upon us, I was
able to view without distraction the terrible devastation wrought upon Tokyo
by our B-29s.

Never in your wildest dreams could you visualize such destruction. There are no houses left standing. Tokyo is a mass of strewn rubble and ashes. Few people walk the deserted streets. The city has an eerie appearance of being a huge ghost town. Actually, Tokyo is no more.

Words of description fail me. You would have to view the nightmarish scene yourself to believe that such devastation could be, not only in Tokyo, but in all the cities where our B-29s paid a visit.

In sharp contrast to the ruins of the great cities is the green countryside, with its rolling, terraced hills, its valleys, rice paddies, and quaint houses with their upturned corners.

Always before in my letters to you I had described the Japanese homeland as being drab, foreboding and colorless. Maybe this description was forthcoming because I was such an unwelcome visitor there. One is not apt to get the proper perspective while looking down the barrels of unfriendly guns which are shooting flak at you. At such times you are definitely not interested in the color and beauty of the terrain below. In reality, the Japanese country is a thing of rare beauty when viewed from the air. Only the eyesores of her burned-out cities mar [her].

Thank God this terrible conflict has been terminated, and now that the war is officially over it shouldn't be long till I return to the U.S.—Happy Day.

Yesterday's "show of power" mission has been generously credited as combat on the records of all who participated. So now I'm credited with 32 combat missions over the Japanese homeland, and I have accrued well in excess of 100 points toward rotation. This record should insure an early return.

Love,
Van

II

•

BONDS

Lloyd Kilmer (left) and Tom Gibbon reunite on "Lloyd Kilmer and Tom Gibbon Day," May 14, 1999.

———————— • ————————

There was never a time in American life when so many people were involved in so many ways in a shared cause. It was impossible not to be affected in some fashion by the war effort, however far you may have been from the front lines.

In that common experience, old ties were strengthened and new ones were formed to last a lifetime. Whatever else may have happened later, World War II was a shared passage of trial and terror, triumph and loss, laughter and reflection. The relationships formed then have been a continuing and reaffirming link to that unique time.

The father of my friend and colleague Tim Russert of *Meet the Press* is a World War II veteran, a B-24 crewman in the 8th Army Air Force. Tim Russert, Sr.—Big Russ, as we call him—has two families: his son and three daughters—and his buddies at the South Buffalo, New York, American Legion Post 721, working-class men who are joined forever by their adventures in what so many of that generation call simply "the war."

In *The Greatest Generation* I wrote about the Dumbos, the dinner and bridge meeting of my parents-in-law and their friends from World War II. It began when the wives formed a mutual support group (although they would never have called it that) to fill the long days while their men were in harm's way in distant places. After the war, when the men came home, the group became a long-running gathering of close friends. It turns out there were an untold number of other gatherings across the land, structured in much the same way. Herb Karner of Broken Arrow, Oklahoma, wrote to my wife's aunt and uncle, Lois and Don Gatchell, in Tulsa, to describe his home-town bridge club, which reminds him of the Dumbos.

Instead of four couples, our group consisted of six couples; we have no spe-

cific name, [but are] generally known as the "bridge club." Our origin was the same: all married couples with men in service overseas, women at home raising family and keeping things rolling. When the men returned, we began a rotational meeting at each home for a home-cooked meal, with the hostess furnishing the meat and others bringing vegetables, salads, and desserts, each contributing their favorite dish. Before the meal, we had a round of drinks. Just one. Remember, liquor was expensive in those days when cash was short. To this day, my wife Ruth's favorite drink is a whiskey sour.

Following the meal we played bridge. We had a custom that when someone went down, the players who lost would put a penny in a pot. The accumulated pot went to the player who drew a 10-high hand. It seems improbable, but at one time the pot got as high as $17. Overzealous bidding, perhaps.

Who are we? I am the oldest by a few months—I will be 84 in June. The youngest is 77. Two were in the Air Corps, one was a B-17 pilot, and I was an aviation ordnance officer. Two were Navy, both serving aboard ships, two were Army, one enlisted, one officer. Sorry, no Marines. But I do have a close tie to the Marines, which is another story. Two of us, of which I am one, also saw combat in Korea, which also is another story.

Today? The group is still together. However, about three years ago we stopped playing bridge, because one of the group died. Heart attack. But those of us who can still get around get together once a month. No longer do the ladies cook. We meet at a local restaurant selected by the host. We still have *one* drink; we visit about children, grandchildren, and great-grandkids, politics, and sports, and we share the latest jokes.

When we returned from service, we all resumed our lives. My wife and I bought a house, as she had been living with her parents. Several of us completed our education and resumed careers in manufacturing, engineering, insurance, retail. I went into the newspaper business after doing other things.

During all this time there have been *no* divorces among the lot of us. Sadly, this is not true of our offspring. As a group we have 13 children; three of us have three, including my wife and me; one has two kids, and two have one each.

Our collective offspring have done well—several divorces, but professionally they include doctors and a variety of other professions and businesses. They have kept out of trouble, and so far our grandchildren are the kind you brag about. We have 10 grandchildren and three great-grands.

Most of us at one time or other have attended a reunion of our old outfit. For the most part, it's fun, but also depressing. Several years ago Ruth and I attended a reunion of the survivors of the Iwo Jima landing (my tie to the

Marines) and when we walked into the hotel lobby she exclaimed, "My goodness, there's nobody here but a bunch of old, gray-haired men!"

Today I am in relatively good health, about 10 pounds over my fighting weight, active in the community and the Broken Arrow Historical Society. I belong to the Downtown Tulsa Kiwanis Club (member for 38 years) and enjoy woodworking, gardening, and photography. On a lesser scale than previously.

But I am proudest that on January 1st my wife and I have been married 61 years!

Please pardon this intrusion into your life. But I was so moved, many times to tears, when reading Brokaw's book that I felt you would understand my impulse to share our experience as a similar "Dumbo" group.

At least I feel better for having written.

I also wrote about the ROMEO Club, a band of veterans who had grown up in the poor Irish-American neighborhoods of Cambridge, Massachusetts, just around the corner from Harvard Yard. "ROMEO" stands for Retired Old Men Eating Out. The eternal leprechauns of the Cambridge ROMEO Club heard from other informal chapters and even had inquiries about whether there was an application process to start a local ROMEO Club.

ONE OF THE JOYS OF THE REACH OF *THE Greatest Generation* is the rekindling of memories and relationships that had faded. I have become particularly fond of John "Lefty" Caulfield, one of the ROMEO Club members, who returned to Harvard and his baseball scholarship after Navy service during the war. Lefty had this evocative letter from a former teammate, Bill Hickey of Midland, Texas.

Dear John,
   I enjoyed the article in the *Harvard Gazette* about you and your contributions to *The Greatest Generation*. I second everything Mr. Brokaw says about

you, and say thank you for doing all you have done. I can remember how helpful you were to me when I was the third-base coach and you were the captain batting .438 (was your average really that high?). You were just as helpful forty years later when I visited my son Patrick at the business school. You haven't changed in forty-eight years and I love that picture of you in the *Gazette*.

What has happened to all those guys I waved around third base (some of whom were thrown out)—Cliff Crosby, John White, Benny Akilian, Sarto Walsh, Ralph Robinson, Tim Wise, John Canepa, Barry Turner—I could go on forever. I can remember my only game appearance was when Stuffy sent me in as a pinch runner against Boston College at their field in the ninth inning with two outs. I was promptly picked off and we lost by one run.

Your career in education is something to be proud of, and raising eight kids is no simple task. Keep on keeping on, John, and if you ever get close to Midland, Texas, Andree and I would love to see you.

EVERY GENERATION HAS A COLLECTIVE memory, a shared experience, but the men and women who went through the Great Depression and World War II were unique in that the events of their lifetime were so inclusive. Children of the sixties may identify with Woodstock or the Chicago 7, with sex, drugs, and rock and roll. But what about the others, who went to Vietnam or voted for Richard Nixon? For that generation the memory screen is divided, but for the Greatest Generation it is a family portrait.

Those bonds take many forms, some of them haunting, painful. Gregory Kirchner, of Bethel Park, Pennsylvania, wrote to share a story he's carried with him since the war, and to ask for help. Kirchner served as a medic with the 76th Infantry Division and has tried for more than fifty years to locate the wife of a soldier he treated on the battlefield. After the war, Kirchner worked for the postal service for thirty-six years and raised

ten children, nine of whom are college graduates.

I consider myself very fortunate to have
survived. When an infantry company
went into combat there were three
medics such as me assigned to it. I out-
lived the first two men assigned with
me to Company I, 417th Infantry Regiment, 76th Infantry Division. I also out-
lived eight replacement medics. When
I was promoted, another man took my
place. He was killed the following
morning.

I have tried without success for over
50 years to locate the family of a man I
treated on the battlefield. This man,
one of five who lost all or part of a leg in
a minefield, lost a leg at the hips. As I
treated him, he said to me, "My God,
what will my wife say?" There he was,
almost blown in half, and he was thinking of her, not himself. This all happened at night during a rainfall. I have
always wanted to let his wife know that
he was thinking of her. This desire has
been renewed when I see the scope of

the research you had to do. His name was Glenn Jones. All I know is he lived in one of the Southern States. Three days before, Glenn had received a letter from his wife stating that she was about to enter the hospital for their first child. He said, "I hope she will be okay." He died in an ambulance on his way to a field hospital.

With the invaluable help of the Veterans Administration we found Sgt. Jones's widow, Virginia, living in a rural area of western North Carolina. She moved there from Winston-Salem to be with her parents and have her child after Glenn Jones was killed. She never remarried.

Virginia was surprised to hear of Gregory Kirchner's letter, since she'd never met anyone who'd served with her husband. She agreed to speak with him on the telephone but asked that he not include any gory details, explaining that even after fifty-four years, "The hurt is still there."

I arranged for Kirchner to call on an autumn Sunday afternoon, and he and Virginia talked for an hour. He said he was "thrilled to have lived so long to finally have found her." Kirchner told Virginia he was not only her husband's medic but also his friend, and he recalled their being on the move and receiving mail from home: "We were reading our letters and Glenn said, 'Well, by now my wife should be entering the hospital for our first baby.' " He also told her how Glenn repeatedly worried about her welfare as he was being treated for his fatal wounds.

As for Virginia, she said their conversation was "almost like getting a message from Glenn." She was particularly pleased that her grandson, who is a history buff, will now be able to read something of a grandfather he never knew.

Virginia said that when her husband was killed, they'd been married ten months and ten days; Glenn, Jr., arrived two months later. She said that her husband would have been proud to know that he had a son carrying his name, adding that although at first she found it difficult to call her son Glenn, after a while she was glad she had named him for his father.

Glenn, Jr., fifty-four, is an engineer with the International Paper company in Wilmington, North Carolina. He was raised by his mother, his grandparents, and his uncles. A few years ago, Virginia gave him a shadow box that contained his father's medals from the war.

Gregory Kirchner told Virginia Jones that another friend of Glenn's, Andrew Patrick of Ohio, was also wounded at the same time and returned home alive but with part of his leg missing. He said he would put them in touch as well.

Fifty-four years after a terrible night in the dark and rain of the Battle of the Bulge, when Sgt. Glenn Jones was mortally wounded, his wife now knows that his final thoughts were of her.

ONE OF THE MOST POIGNANT STORIES in *The Greatest Generation* involved Jeanette Gagne Norton, who lost her husband, Camille, during the war. Camille, a paratrooper with the 82nd Airborne, was awarded the Silver Star posthumously for his heroism during the battle of Nijmegen, a critical crossing point between Holland and Germany. He died without ever seeing his son, Bob. After Jeanette's story appeared, she unexpectedly heard from one of Camille's closest friends from the service. She recounted:

This man, Clarence Ollum, went to Fort Benning, Georgia, jump school the same time my husband did. They went over to North Africa together, and then to Sicily. He made all the same jumps my husband did—all four of them. The last jump, of course, was where my husband didn't make it. But Clarence, who's called Bud, came back with another of my husband's buddies, Vic, and they made it a mission to find me and my boy because my husband, Camille, was always talking about me and showing them pictures of me. So they said when they got back they'd see if they could find Gagne's wife and boy. But in the course of time I remarried, and my name changed, you see. So in the course of fifty years they'd been looking for me and my boy. And of course they never found us. Vic died a few years ago.

But Bud had been telling this friend of his, Steve, "I looked for Jeanette and her boy for years and was never able to find them." He even showed him pictures of Camille. But then Steve got a copy of Mr. Brokaw's book, and he called Bud and said, "I think there's a story in here that sounds like it might be your buddy." Bud saw Camille's picture and said, "Oh my God, that's Gagne!" He was just so taken aback. And so Steve brought him over here and I met him, and it . . . oh my goodness. It was wonderful. All the things I'd always wondered about, like the different places where my husband was—his letters were censored, naturally—this Bud has been able to fill me in on, on things I never knew about. Like what it was like to jump out of the plane, and what my husband was like, and whether he was nervous. "Well, of course he was," Bud said, "just like the rest of us. We always wondered if each jump would be our last."

So I can ask him anything and he tells me. He didn't see my husband when he got killed, but he heard about it. He said to me, "I almost feel guilty because I came back and your husband didn't." And I said, "Oh, don't feel bad, Bud, it could have just as well been you." Can you imagine. . . . He showed me the same identical picture of my husband as the one in the book. On October fifteenth, I'm going to Atlanta to a Company E reunion, where I'll be meeting whoever is left of my husband's company. If it hadn't been for the book, I never would have met this gentleman. And you can't imagine how happy that's made him—and how happy it's made me!

W. E. BILDERBACK, JR., OF FORT WORTH, Texas, a businessman who deals in construction supplies and equipment, wrote about a letter taken from a dead Japanese soldier at Iwo Jima. Reading a translation of the letter fifty years later helped change his views about the Japanese.

During World War II, I was a first lieutenant in anti-aircraft artillery. I made the invasion of Iwo Jima with the Marine Corps.

One night at Iwo Jima, a lot of Japanese soldiers were killed. The next morning, one of my sergeants told me he had taken a letter from one of the dead soldiers and asked if I would like to have it. I said yes, I would.

Fifty years later, on a trip to Maui, I had the letter translated by a young woman at the Kapalua Bay Hotel. When my wife read me the letter, I cried. It could have been written to me by my own wife. I detested the Japanese at the time the letter was written, because I had been taken from my new bride and a promising career. But this letter made me realize that the dead soldier didn't want to be in Iwo Jima either.

The young woman who translated the letter was so emotional she cried. She asked if I would mind if she kept the letter and tried to locate the Japanese wife. A year later, the widow was found and presented with the letter.

This is the letter to Mr. Bilderback from the Japanese soldier's wife, Yoshi Sakuma:

I would like to express my sincere appreciation for all your and Ms. Egi's [the translator's] recent efforts on my behalf. I received the letter of memento written to my late husband, in the presence of the mayor of Funehiki Town and officials from the Fukushima prefectural government and Funehiki Town. Though Mr. William Bilderback does not understand Japanese, he kept the letter which was entrusted to him during the Second World War over 50 years ago. I truly feel that this letter reminds us that all the people living on the Earth can be united as one, despite the conflicts we have endured through history. I read the letter again and again and I felt that my late husband had finally come back to us after 51 years. I was flooded with a thousand emotions and tears.

As soon as I received the letter, I visited his grave to tell him of this matter. Before the war, I lived with my late husband and two daughters happily in the vicinity of the Joban coal mine. However, he was called into the army and fell in battle in Iwo Jima island. I was at my wits' end and I came back to my parents' home with my daughters. However, my youngest daughter passed away due to illness shortly thereafter. I started work as a laborer, but we earned a precarious living.

I remarried and lived with my second husband and my daughter's family and my two granddaughters for a while, and now my two granddaughters have married and I am blessed with four great-grandchildren. I am 80 years old now and I enjoy practicing gateball every day for the gateball competitions held three times annually. We live happily on a small old-age pension provided by the National Pension System of Japan.

I believe that your and Ms. Yuriko Egi's thoughtfulness, which transcends national boundaries, will contribute to building stronger ties of friendship and this will be passed down for posterity from generation to generation.

Please take care of yourselves and I wish you a peaceful life.

Bilderback also sent a copy of the letter written by Mrs. Sakuma to her husband when he was a soldier on Iwo Jima:

It's been a long time; hope you are fine as usual. When you left home it was a cold day with white clouds, but now spring has come and it's already in the month of May, with fresh green leaves. How fast the time flies!

I am fine, too, protecting family back here. Nariko is fine and growing up without catching any cold or flu.

Every morning when I say a prayer for you, Nariko also imitates me to pray with her little hands together. I think of you often and pray a lot for you. When I ask Nariko where her father is, she answers "Banzai" with both her arms up in the air. Even though she is little she does not forget.

Good-bye from your wife.

LORRAINE DAVIS OF SPANISH FORK, UTAH, was born in 1926, so her earliest memories are of the Great Depression. As she says, "I did not know life wasn't supposed to be poor. Older siblings remember better times." By the time Lorraine was in high school, the war was on and her life took another turn. She begins by describing a bus trip she took to Salt Lake City shortly after graduating.

I sat with a former classmate who had been home on leave and was going back to Salt Lake to be sent overseas with the Marines. We talked about many things, but not his future. . . . Suddenly, an eighteen-year-old girl matured several years.

Now I want to tell you about the "girls who were left behind." Some girls married and were left alone. The rest of us were left alone, too, since all the young men were in the service. We began meeting every week or two for companionship and support. We talked about husbands, boyfriends and the war. Every day was much the same. We were all expected to get a job to help the war effort. Many worked in munitions plants or other war-related industries. Some were even "Rosie the Riveter." I started to work for the USDA a few days after graduation. Every day was about the same as we came home from work to listen to the evening news or to see it on the newsreels at the movies. Many letters were written to places all over the world. I corresponded with many young men in every part of the world since I did not have anyone special. I saved the letters for a few years and finally discarded them. Now, I wish I had not.

This same group of girls are still meeting after 55 years. After the war, boyfriends and husbands came home; the rest of us married, and we all started having those "Baby Boomers." Soon they were going to school, enjoying high school activities, getting married, and having families of their own and even grandchildren. All of this time, "the girls" were still meeting every month, supporting each other, caring for each other, and becoming even closer. At first we called ourselves the Club of '44. We later changed the name to Amity because we were such good friends. Some have passed away, but we still have close to 25 members. The only prerequisite for membership is to have been a member of the class of 1944. Amity is a consequence of World War II.

WORLD WAR II WAS A GREAT EQUALIZER. Poor kids and sons of privilege were side by side in the foxhole or bomber cockpit; Texas cowboys and street-smart toughs from Brooklyn depended on each other to stay alive; Harvard graduates learned from high school dropouts. George Chiungos of Weston, Massachusetts, shared a story about the bond between his father and a surgeon he knew during the Normandy invasion.

I recently purchased your book, *The Greatest Generation,* and was absolutely amazed as I began to read it. My father died at the age of 44 in 1963, but I can still remember the stories that he told regarding his wartime experiences in North Africa, Sicily, Italy and, of course, D-Day. He was a medic who landed sometime on that first day, and I can only imagine the horror and carnage that he witnessed. As I reflect upon his stories, he never spoke of the horrors of the war. Instead, he talked incessantly about the lasting friendships he developed, and many of the photographs in my possession today reveal wartime camaraderie, time spent with the children and other residents of any particular town or village in which his Company happened to be at any given time, and the like. In fact, I am in possession of a photo taken by a Utah

Beach café owner and his wife that later became part of a Normandy postcard depicting my father and a friend relaxing on Utah Beach shortly after the Invasion. The café owner . . . billed them as the first two Americans to land on Utah Beach on D-Day. Clearly, this was somewhat of an exaggeration, but not by much! I had the opportunity to visit this family in 1972 and sat in their café while the owner and his wife tried to communicate their feelings about what my father and the American soldiers in general meant to them. I look very much like my father, and I can still remember so vividly the café owner, Felix, pointing to the original photo of my father and his friend that was hanging on the wall of the café and then pointing to me with tears streaming down his face. . . .

I will close with a story that will stay with me forever and reinforces much of what you present in your book about this incredible generation. My father learned in early 1961 that one Dr. Ballantine was senior neurologist at Massachusetts General Hospital. He had always marveled at Dr. Ballantine's incredible battlefield neurosurgical skills, as he had served in Dr. Ballantine's unit and witnessed field surgical miracles too numerous to recount. My father owned and operated a dairy products processing business. One day, he took it upon himself to drive into Boston to deliver several tubs of specialty Greek cheeses to Dr. Ballantine and renew his acquaintance. My father was taken aback by Dr. Ballantine's surprise and shock that someone would actually do that, as he simply wanted to express his admiration for what he had seen Dr. Ballantine do under some incredible conditions in Normandy. Two years later, my father was stricken with a triple brain aneurysm and requested that Dr. Ballantine perform the operation. The operation was a success, but his heart gave out and he died shortly thereafter. Dr. Ballantine's team of eight medical specialists operated for ten hours. When the uninsured portion of the bill arrived at our house (some $25,000 in 1963!), it was marked "paid-in-full" with a warm, personal note to the family from Dr. Ballantine remarking, among other things, on the impact on him of the surprise visit by my father two years earlier.

DURING THE WAR AND IMMEDIATELY after, Hollywood movies often included this scene: a tough, battle-scarred G.I. befriending a waif, a young European victim of the long years of upheaval. It was not just the screenwriters' imagination. Many veterans recounted their memories of children and families they met in the war zones.

Yves Masson, who now lives in San Rafael, California, was a child in Paris when the Allies arrived.

I was an eight-year-old little boy when the courageous men you wrote about came to liberate me and the French capital. Of course, like all those who were there, I have very dear memories of the time: the evening when all the church bells of Paris tolled at the same time after having been silent all the years of the German occupation; the parades, the joy and the relief from fear.

In spite of all the hardships, dangers, triumphs and despairs that they had been through, so far from their land, these soldiers were so gentle. One took me on his tank and talked in a language I did not know, but his smile and his laugh made me happy; some gave me candy (the first candy I ever remember). They took me by the hand and walked with me. I was then too young to comprehend the scale of the accomplishment of the American armies, but I loved these men. I have read many books since then and know of all the battles and the great victories. The memories of those moments in late August 1944 remained vivid, yet, until I read your book, they had a dream-like quality.

It is because of this encounter with the men of the greatest generation that at the age of 29, when I had the chance,

I came to America. Now a citizen, I have the privilege to live in this wonderful land.

What your book has done for me is to bridge the gap between the nameless heroes who so profoundly changed my life and the people whom I live with every day. Now these heroes are no longer part of a dream-like remembrance, they have names. Some, of course, I know because of their accomplishments in the past decades but I did not know they were there. Others, less famous, now have a name, a place where they live, and family. I may have met some of them. The word "closure" is overused in these days of stress and complexity. But in this case your book did close out that episode of my life by bringing it beyond the blind admiration and the treasured recollection to the reality of today's life in America with people I meet every day.

THE BONDS OF WORLD WAR II REACH across the years and even across generations. L'Myra Hoogland of Owatonna, Minnesota, knew little of her father's final days—until she found his best friend.

I, too, am a child of that generation, but I am also an orphan of one of its soldiers. My father, Myron (Mike) B. Anderson, was one of the multitude of casualties of the Battle of the Bulge on December 16, 1944. He was killed two months before I was born on February 9, 1945.

My dad was one of the "older" G.I.s. The age limit had been lifted or raised. He was a 30-year-old from a small Scandinavian farming community called Gunder, in N.E. Iowa. He drove a truck, dreaming of having a larger trucking business. But it was not to be.

He has always been part of my life, especially in my deepest thoughts: "Would he be proud of me? Would he approve of my choices? What would he do?" And oh, I wish he knew my husband and had been able to love his grandchildren. . . .

My mother survived all this trauma. . . . She taught elementary school for 41 years while raising me—no welfare or help in those years. She shared her work ethic with me—just as your parents did you and all of us. She's quite a lady.

We both have been blessed, and perhaps me most of all in the last six years or so. I have met my dad's best friend, Duncan Truman from Warwick, New York, and through him others of my dad's Army buddies of the 424th AT division of the 106th Army. He and others have added information more precious than gold. Though I knew, for so long, as much as my family, he and the others have willingly shared memories of horror and honor. Until I wrote him five years ago he thought my dad was alive. It is through him that I have written to and talked to the officer my dad drove a jeep for. This is all 53 years after his death. God has blessed me through these men and their memories. Aren't we blessed?

CAUGHT IN THE MIDDLE WERE THE civilians, especially those in countries directly in the path of Hitler's ambitions. The Belgians had not a moment of peace for five years, and Belgian families were often as brave as the most heroic soldier. Christine Winchester lives in La Grange Park, Illinois, but because of what happened to her grandfather she has another family in Belgium.

My grandfather was a bomber pilot who had been shot down. His crew, with the exception of his navigator and himself, bailed out and were picked up by the Allies. When Grandpa went down, trying for his alternate target, several young children helped him get away from the German search party. To make a long story short, he was an escapee/evader for 9 months. A man named Emile VanVeerMeyes and [his] family hid him from the Germans at risk of their own lives for 6 of those months, while he recovered from injuries. When Grandpa snuck out just before a raid, he was picked up and spent another 9 months in a POW prison in Ghent. During this time Emile kept up with how he was doing.

Even now, 50+ years away from this event, Emile and his wife and Grandma and Grandpa see each other almost every year, and are in constant correspondence. Louise and Emile are godparents to some of us, and have come to everybody's weddings, christenings, etc., for as long as I can remember. They are truly a part of our family, for without them, none of us would exist.

MARYANNE CERRA OF DAVIE, FLORIDA, has another version of the familiar story of an American G.I. and a young victim of the war.

My dad, Major Riccardi, is the child of immigrant parents from Italy. During WWII, my grandparents had five sons on active duty. My dad was stationed in Italy as a bombardier, and his daily bombing missions were over the land of his parents.

One of the many poignant stories my dad has shared was one of a little Italian boy named Mario, who, during the war, would hang out at the barracks helping the G.I.'s in hopes of earning a nickel or piece of food to share with his family. My dad took Mario and his family under his wing. Before his daily missions my dad would teach Mario several English words and then review them when he returned. After several months, my dad was transferred and eventually lost touch with Mario.

On the 40th anniversary of the end of WWII, my dad organized the first reunion of the 454th Bomb Squadron and amazingly was able to locate over 500 men. (The reunion continues yearly.) Incredibly, one of the men had Mario's address. On a subsequent trip to Italy my parents were able to meet with a delighted Mario and his family, but it was not until I traveled to Italy that I realized the impact of those long-ago English lessons. Mario is now the manager of two hotels, and in fluent English he told me that had it not been for my father's influence and lessons, he would have been "a bum" (his words) and his life was forever changed.

LLOYD KILMER, A POOR MINNESOTA farm boy who went on to fly B-24s during the war, was shot down and captured. One of his most vivid memories was of the day an American tank broke through the prison walls to free him. Fifty-four years later he made a new friend.

A couple of weeks ago a fellow called and said he was reading "the BOOK" about the 14th Armored Division of Patton's Third Army liberating Stalag 7A on April 29, 1945. He said that he was the commander on the tank that came through the barbed wire that day—and I was on his tank!!! He was my liberator.

After several conversations with Tom Gibbon of Palm Springs, California, we decided to drive over and meet Tom and his wife, Chris. We drove over last Thursday, and he had arranged for a motel for us. Upon arrival, we called Tom and they met us in the lobby of the motel. When they arrived—newspaper photographers and reporters were on hand. What a joyous meeting—big story on the front page of the paper, with a color picture. He took a group of us for a very special dinner.

They picked us up after breakfast to go to the Air Force museum for an 11:00 A.M. TV press conference. Several POWs showed up after reading the piece in the morning paper. It was a time of telling old war stories and presenting of gifts to each other. I was presented with a PROCLAMATION OF THE CITY OF PALM SPRINGS declaring May 14, 1999, to be Lloyd Kilmer and Tom Gibbon Day. Next, a "Certificate of Special Congressional Recognition" signed by Mary Bono, member of Congress (Sonny Bono's widow), and then a beautiful walnut plaque from the Narconnon International Board of Governors, their first "WE'RE NOT DONE YET!" award.

After lunch, we all took a couple of hours to rest before a reception for us with 25 or 30 people attending. Again, a time for fun and telling old war stories. After supper, we were ready to go to our motel room.

Tom and Chris came to the motel after breakfast to wish us a safe trip home. It was, and we are really looking forward to them visiting us. What a fantastic couple of days!

EVEN WHEN THE WAR WAS OVER IN THE Pacific, not all of the American troops were able to return home. They became part of the occupation army that moved into Japan under the command of General MacArthur. George Zimmermann, a Marine, sent me a story he wrote for a recent edition of *Leatherneck*, the Marine magazine.

It was Aug. 6, 1945, the day the first atomic bomb exploded on Hiroshima,

Japan. Three days later, the city of Nagasaki on the southernmost island of Kyushu was destroyed by [an atomic bomb almost twice as powerful as] the Hiroshima bomb. Japan surrendered, and victory was declared on Aug. 15 by the Allies. The war was over, and we Marines of the Eighth Marine Regiment rejoiced at the thought of going home.

But our joy was short-lived.

Many of us found out that we would not be going home. Instead we learned that we had been assigned as part of the occupation force in Japan.

We learned Japanese phrases and customs and studied maps and photographs to help us find our way through Nagasaki to our billet near the town of Kumamoto.

When we landed, we were awed by the destruction. The city looked nothing like the pictures we had studied.

Eventually, word of an orphanage in the city began making its way around the base. Forty girls, mostly under the age of 6, were cared for by two French nuns, an elderly but spry Mother Superior Marguerite and a younger assistant, Sister Saint Paul. These women were helped by six Japanese nuns who had been raised at the orphanage.

Marines began spending their leave time at the orphanage helping the nuns and entertaining the children. Dressed in beautiful kimonos, the girls sang Japanese songs for us, and we taught them English songs such as "Oh! Suzannah," "Silent Night" and "Jingle Bells." We played games like jump rope and Blind Man's Buff with them in the orphanage courtyard.

The 8th Marines adopted the orphans for Christmas in 1945. The cook and his crew whipped up a complete turkey dinner while other leathernecks found a fir tree, which everyone decorated with hundreds of painted paper ornaments.

On one visit I asked Mother about a 16-year-old girl, named Miako, who sat by herself and never participated in anything, not even communion. The other children had said Miako had a mental problem, but Mother told me that the girl simply could not speak or hear. She lived in a silent world all her own.

As a teenager, I learned the universal sign language, which uses hand gestures for words and finger combinations for letters. I spent an hour each visit teaching Miako how to sign, and her vocabulary and knowledge of the alphabet increased steadily.

Since she knew no language at all, we were working with a blank slate. I would point to an object such as a flag and then show her one sign for the word flag as well as the signs for the letters of the word. She learned her name and the names of the nuns and some of her friends. Soon I was able to ask her what she did or ate or wanted and whether she was feeling happy, sad, angry or sick.

One small girl always took Miako's hand to help her participate in games and daily activities, and since this child already knew the alphabet and many English words, she was taught sign language as well.

Miako's silent world soon began to explode with conversation as even the nuns began to pick up some signs and communicate with her.

I was discharged in July, and while I was home for Christmas in 1946 and happy to be back with my family, I would never forget how my fellow Marines conquered boredom and homesickness by the love we shared with the nuns and the children.

To this day, I wonder what became of that little deaf girl. Did she get an education? Did she get married? Did she accomplish great things? I guess I'll never know.

JIM DIBBLE OF PORT JEFFERSON, NEW York, grew up knowing that an uncle had been a fighter pilot and was killed during a mission over Italy. Then he had a life-changing experience when he visited an Ohio museum.

My uncle, . . . 1st Lt. James P. Dibble, was a fighter pilot with the 94th Fighter Squadron, 1st Fighter Group during World War II. On September 9, 1943, while strafing a German convoy moving up to attack the Americans landing at Salerno, Jim was shot down by ground fire and killed.

At the time it was reported to his wife that he was last seen in his parachute and declared missing in action. One year later, with no further information, he was presumed dead. In October 1946 the Army wrote saying Jim's remains had been identified and buried in Naples, Italy. He was subsequently returned to the United States and was buried in Middleville, Michigan, in December 1948.

This was all anyone knew. For many years, questions about Jim and his last mission lingered. Everyone doubted that we would ever really know how Jim met his fate. There was even doubt that, in fact, it was Jim who had returned to Michigan.

During 1986 I was visiting the U.S. Air Force Museum in Dayton, Ohio. On the wall hung a picture of a group of men from the 1st Fighter Group in North Africa being addressed by Eddie Rickenbacker, World War I's top American ace, then a member of the 94th Aero Squadron. Was it possible that my uncle was in the picture, or was at least present? I decided the time had come to try to learn everything I could.

Over the next 13 years I went from knowing very little to knowing the details of every mission flown and everything about Jim's last flight; and, yes, he had met Eddie Rickenbacker the day of the photograph.

On September 9, 1943, both my uncle and his wingman were shot down. The wingman, Stan Wojick, was reported to have crashed with his plane. What really happened was that Stan had bailed out and Jim had crash-landed. Stan was captured and sent to a POW camp and subsequently liberated by the Russians in 1945. Jim was shot by the Germans following his crash landing and was buried next to his plane by two brothers, Vito and Paolo Cimino, who were working in the field at the time of the crash. Jim became an unknown soldier because all personal items had been removed by the Germans. It wasn't until after the war, when Stan had been accounted for and the crashed plane identified as Jim's, that an identification was possible.

When I started out to learn about my uncle, I wanted to learn what had happened on that mission. Along the way I found his crew chief, who had taken a picture of Jim standing in front of his plane on September 5, 1943. The Air Force sent me a slew of medals, none of which we knew he had been awarded. I discovered he had been nominated for the Distinguished Flying Cross, and after we fulfilled all the requirements outlined by the Secretary of the Air

Force, in 1990 a formal ceremony was held at the Wright Patterson Air Force Base, with my father accepting the medal for the family. I met the pilots he flew with, sat in a P-38 fighter, and now, after searching the crash site, I have pieces of the P-38 that Jim sat in. It has been an incredible journey.

However, more important, I learned something I had not expected to. I learned about the character of the man. Character was what your book was all about, and that's why it meant so much to me. It really helped me to put into focus not only the value of the years it took to learn about Jim, but [also] the value of what he and his fellow pilots have done for those of us living in this world today.

On August 31st Jim wrote to his wife, "Yesterday I achieved the top spot in flying combat, I led the First Fighter Group into combat. I was a little nervous when confronted with the responsibility, but I just did my best and I guess it was good enough." The mission will long be remembered for the group's skill, daring and sacrifice in successfully defending a flight of B-26 bombers to and from their target area without a single bomber being lost to an overwhelming German fighter attack of over 100 planes.

On September 9, 1943, Jim flew his 49th and final mission. While strafing a German convoy he made the supreme sacrifice. His fate is no longer a mystery. We are comforted by the thought that Jim died doing what he enjoyed most, leading fighter pilots into combat. Jim didn't try to be a hero. He didn't have to. Good officers are good officers, whatever the reward.

I have learned a lot about the 94th Fighter Squadron in North Africa during the early stages of the war. I have learned a lot about my uncle, his training, his life in North Africa, and his combat missions. But the most important thing I have learned was about the character it took for these very young men to assume the responsibilities that

they did and accomplish what they did.
It is truly remarkable.

LURA M. WADE OF SHAWNEE MISSION,
Kansas, wrote about her husband, who was
taken prisoner under circumstances similar
to those of Jim Dowling, whom I introduced
in *The Greatest Generation.*

I . . . was amazed when I was reading
about James Dowling and saw on page
48 how he was shot down, taken by
train to Stalag Luft I near Barth, Germany, and eventually liberated by Rus-
sian troops in May 1945.

This is *so* like what happened to my
husband, Rollin Wade, and is the first
time I've ever seen anything about a fellow POW in Stalag Luft I. We were unable to take the trip there in the 1980s.

We were married after the war, on 18
August 1946, and he never talked about
his war experiences until about 10 years
ago, when I, working on the family ge-
nealogy, persuaded him to write his

memoirs. Also, I heard about the POW medals and wanted to get one for him, so I wrote our senator Bob Dole, who arranged for him to get one. It was a surprise to Rollin when it came in the mail, but I think he was pleased to have it. He always said he shouldn't be rewarded for getting captured. He was a liaison pilot for the field artillery when he was shot down and when his plane came down he was surrounded by German troops with machine guns, so had no chance to get away. He was at Stalag Luft I for 11 months, and said the Russians who liberated them were drinking vodka and loud.

In camp he kept a notebook where he wrote down many things, from books he read in camp to cooking utensils they made from whatever was available (he made drawings of these things), names of fellow prisoners, etc. My family treasures this little book, which I found after he died suddenly on 7 July 1992, three days after his 77th birthday on the 4th of July.

We have 4 children, 9 grandchildren aged from 8 to 28, and 2 precious great-grandsons. I so wish he was still here to enjoy these little boys.

My generation (I am 77) did what we needed to do and had values and morals that seem not as important nowadays, at least to some people. I am thankful for all my memories of the experiences of my lifetime, and that my two brothers and Rollin survived the war.

IN *THE GREATEST GENERATION* I WROTE about Martha Putney, an African American woman who left her small Pennsylvania town and joined the Army in search of opportunity. She recently received this letter from a former high school classmate.

September 3, 1999
Dear Martha,

It is with great pleasure that I congratulate you for your accomplishments and success in life, in spite of the barricades that were in your way. While looking at the table of contents in *The Greatest Generation,* I saw the name Martha Settle Putney. It went through my mind that there can only be one person named Martha Settle. I turned to the chapter and I was right, it was you.

I was Peg Fenimore, class of '35, N.H.S. I remember you well, we were in several classes together. That was another time, I was not fully aware of the struggles that your race had to face. I have come a long way since then.

I have had a good life, mostly handed to me. There have been ups and downs. The blessings are a good father, mother, and siblings and a healthy, devoted son and daughter. Some of the downs are a divorce at age 33 and widowed at age 50.

For many years I taught, first elementary school, then learning-disabled and socially & emotionally disturbed. Which were all very gratifying.

Now I am retired but work part-time at Montpelier, the home of James Madison. I volunteer at the Orange Visitors Bureau and tutor special-ed. children.

I live with my daughter, Cindy, in Orange. I enjoy good health for which I am most grateful.

I hope you are enjoying your retirement and are in good health. If you get down this way, do give me a call.

Congratulations and best wishes to you.

Fondly,
Peg Fenimore Aspden O'Connor
Orange, VA

III

———— • ————

LOSS

Ralph Stewart's grave.

TO OUR DEAR LIBERATORS
MEMORIAL DAY 1946

The crew of Lieutenant Roland Matthew Cocker's PBM plane, April 7, 1945 (Cocker is in the back row, third from the left).

———————•———————

Now, more than a half-century after the end of World War II, those years have a kind of rosy glow for many. The stylish wardrobes; the handsome young men in uniform; swing music, conspicuous patriotism, and a just cause. The snappy patter of Bob Hope and the soothing baritone of Bing Crosby, the boogie-woogie of the Andrews Sisters, the jazz of Duke Ellington, Glenn Miller's distinctive melodies—all are on the sound track of the memories running across the mind's eye.

However, the stark reality is that 292,131 Americans were killed in action in World War II. They lie in lovingly tended cemeteries in France and Belgium, in the Philippines and Hawaii, in their hometown family plots and in unmarked graves where they fell in distant battle. To walk among those headstones, reading the names, ages, military units, and home states of the dead, is a humbling and simultaneously affirming experience. Most who died were very young and very far from home. Now, think of those who were left behind—the parents, wives, girlfriends, and children. Their loss is not a fleeting experience; it endures well beyond emotional visits to a cemetery.

So many young men left home at a tender age—late teens or early twenties—and were never seen again. Now the only reminder is a yellowing black-and-white photograph of a sailor in a new uniform, or a Marine on a sandy beach, or an airman with a crushed cap set at a jaunty angle, or a soldier looking at once proud and not old enough to be a warrior. Someone's son, brother, husband, boyfriend, died in a way that even now is too painful to recount easily.

Most of those who survived know it was simply fate that saved them. Their buddies a few feet to the left and to the right were fatally wounded. The survivors carry that with them to this day; they are still asking, "Why did I survive?" Every day and every opportunity is a dividend their fallen comrades never realized. One man wrote to me about his father, a World War II combat veteran who had lost many young friends in battle. Recalling those who didn't live beyond their twenties, the dying man said to his son, "Don't sing any sad songs for me, boy. I've had my life. I've seen my grandchildren. Don't sing any sad songs for me."

I'VE TOLD YOU ABOUT JEANETTE GAGNE Norton, whose first husband, Camille Gagne, survived D-Day but died later in the battle for Nijmegen. He never saw their son. When the war was over, Jeanette said, "Everybody was honking their horns and yelling . . . but I couldn't really join in. . . . My heart wasn't in it."

Anne Black, now a corporate executive in Washington, D.C., was born after her father was killed in the closing months of the war. She writes eloquently of the effect on her mother, her own childhood, and their later years together.

My parents, Ceal and Ed Moloney, had been childhood friends in Englewood,

New Jersey. They fell in love in their 20s but, because of the Depression, postponed their wedding till their early 30s, the coming war propelling them into action. During the four years of their marriage, my parents lived with my maternal grandmother in Englewood; my father enlisted early on in the war and was an MP on the docks in New York.

In January 1945, with the end of the war in sight and my mother four months pregnant, my father, at the "ancient" age of 34, was called overseas as part of the mop-up effort as the Allies moved across Europe. He was a sergeant in the 273rd Infantry Regiment, 69th Infantry Division. On April 14, he was killed in action near Aachen, Germany.

One of his buddies wrote, "We were attacking an A.A. [antiaircraft] position and 88s opened up on us. We were pretty far out from the town and we got orders to withdraw. Ed was at least 300 to 500 yards out front. On my way back,

I noticed a medic working on one of our boys but with the 88s still coming, I didn't stop to look. When the medics got back, they told us it was Ed who had got it. They said, 'He never knew what hit him.' "

Six weeks later, while the world was rejoicing at the end of the war in Europe, I was born in New York. About to leave the hospital, my mother wrote the following to her brother: "I have neglected to write you lately but I've lost whatever pep I ever had. . . . The baby arrived on May 26 and I hope this kid has been born under a luckier star than Ed and I were. She weighed 9 lbs. and 8 ozs., so I did pretty good for an old dame. Mother is so nervous lately that she can't keep her hands still. Guess I haven't helped much with all the weeping, but I can't help it. I miss Ed so much, I can't imagine what I'll ever do, and can't find much reason for breathing. Everybody tells me that now I have the baby I'll feel better, but they don't know what they're talking about."

My mother had lost everything she was waiting for. She lost her dreams. There were an awful lot of perfect linen tablecloths in our house that never got used. So many things being saved for a future that was never to be.

And then there was me, born in the wake of my father's death, yet ready for life. I grew up living with my mother, grandmother and an ongoing parade of cats and dogs. I had a loving, stable childhood. I was close to my aunts and uncle on my mother's side and I had fun with my many cousins. I was also very close to my father's family—his brother, aunts, uncles, and my one cousin. And then there were my father's many friends and war buddies who kept in touch with my mother over the years as best they could, sometimes just dropping into her office to chat, to see how things were going.

Growing up, it seemed to me that everyone else came from nice, perfect families made up of a mother, father and children. But, for my mother and

me, our family was just the two of us. I
always felt a strong need to protect her
from unhappiness. On the subject of
my father's death, there was for the
most part silence. For me, this silence
led to feelings of great shame. Shame
that I did not have a father, shame that
he had been killed when everyone else
came home, shame that we'd been left
behind, shame that we were "different."

I was a freshman in college when
President Kennedy was assassinated.
His death was a turning point in my life
because it initiated a mourning for my
own father—something I had never
done. Three years later I went to Europe for the first time and found my
way to my father's grave at the Netherlands American Cemetery at Mar-
graten, Holland. After all these years,
we were finally in the same place at the
same time. He really had existed. It was
good to know where he was at long last.

One morning in 1992, while sitting in
my kitchen drinking a cup of coffee, I
read in the *Washington Post* about a

group of WWII "orphans" laying a wreath in Arlington Cemetery in honor of their fathers' sacrifices. I had only known one other person who had lost her father in the war and it was startling for me to read the interviews. People talking about how, as children, they had imagined that someday their dads would come home, having been held captive in some foreign country all these years. People recalling how no one ever talked about their father's death. And a woman named Ann Mix saying that for years she and her brother had always thought that when they said their prayers, "Our Father who art in Heaven" meant *their* father. I sat and cried my eyes out.

The next day, with the help of the *Post,* I was able to contact Ann Mix and her wonderful organization, the American World War II Orphans Network (AWON). My life then changed forever—and for the good. I found others who were like me. Over the years, I have made good friends, friends with whom WWII is now just part of the conversation. And the shame has mostly gone away, because now, at last, we've finally talked about it—and some days even laughed about it.

I am proud of my dad, and proud of what he did. My dearest wish is that I could have held my dad's hand, looked into his eyes and heard his voice—just once. But that was not to be.

My father left a legacy of love, good humor, courage and standing up for what you believe in. Mom carried on without him, leading a productive life, working until she was 87 and retiring (finally!) to live near me in Washington. At 90, she is with it, reads two papers daily, does some volunteer work and is eager to visit all the sights the city has to offer. From time to time, she dreams of my father vividly. She misses him always.

SOME OF THE WORLD WAR II ORPHANS have spent years trying to determine the circumstances of their father's death and to understand the meaning of the loss in their own lives. Patricia Gaffney-Ansel of New Haven, Connecticut, was born three months after her father went down with his plane in New Guinea.

I am one of more than 183,000 war orphans who belong to the portrait of Americans heralded in *The Greatest Generation*. Most of us have lived with unanswered questions and unresolved grief; many of us have buried the pain deep within our hearts; some of us have sought a way to free the tears in order to heal. I've been given an extraordinary gift . . . a Journey of the Heart.

On March 11, 1944, my twenty-three-year-old father, Second Lieutenant George P. Gaffney, Jr., flew with the 41st Fighter Squadron on a bombing mission to Wewak, New Guinea. Instead of returning to his base, he landed at Saidor to refuel, where he filed a flash report saying he'd shot down an enemy plane and requested to have his

P-47 Thunderbolt checked for damage. At 2:50 P.M. he left the airdrome heading for Gusap, a thirty-minute flight over the Finisterre mountains, and disappeared forever.

Three months later, on the day FDR signed the G.I. Bill into law, I was born a fatherless child. Fate had intervened so I would know my father only as a sepia-toned portrait of a young man in uniform, confined within a picture frame. His silence has been deafening. Although my mother spoke of him and my grandparents searched for him in my face, I could never hear that man in the picture. . . .

Several times during my childhood, the suitcase containing my father's belongings was opened. Mother would talk about him as we held his precious letters and the few personal effects that had been returned from New Guinea after he disappeared. It seems I've always known about the Finisterre mountains, the Ramu river, Saidor and Gusap, as well as the men who'd shared his tent and would later share his fate. . . .

I saw Grandpa Gaffney for the last time in 1970. As I turned to leave him, he asked if I had ever heard from my father. It broke my heart to tell him no. It was a desperate question from a dying man and remains as the saddest moment of my life.

On a morning in September 1993, in my 50th year of life and his death, one of those rare moments occurred when you know things have changed forever. I heard that the wreck of a WWII plane had been recovered in New Guinea. I thought, "Is that the crackle of static penetrating the long, dark silence? Is it meant for me?"

In May 1995 . . . I went to Papua New Guinea, as it had been known since gaining independence twenty years earlier. I passed through a time warp as our plane broke out of the clouds over the lush green grave of the man in the picture. On Mother's Day in America, pilot Richard Leahy and I flew to Gusap, where I buried a box filled with symbols of love in the kunai grass next to the airstrip to which my father had not returned. I listened for the sound of the breeze blowing through the kunai as he had described it in his last letter. I imagined his tent near the Ramu river. I was in a dream. . . .

In November 1996, a letter came from Bruce Hoy, an Australian WWII wreck researcher, saying he had information that could lead to my father's wreck site. Soon after, my quest came to the attention of Alfred Hagen, a Philadelphia businessman who'd been to PNG [Papua New Guinea] searching for the wreckage of his great-uncle, who was lost in 1943. I asked him to look for my father and sent him the Missing Air Crew Report [MACR] which includes the numbers stamped on the engine and [the] eight .50-caliber guns in the wings—*just in case*. . . .

Hagen returned to New Guinea in June 1998. He finally located the wreckage of his great-uncle's plane and then flew back to the Finisterres to continue searching for my father's wreck site. [Local] villagers led him to [a] second site. He identified the wreck as a P-47 but was unable to determine if it was my father's. He did find fragmentary evidence of remains in the cockpit area. It was, as Leahy was to fax later that day, "at the right address." We had reason to hope. The wreck was found at an altitude of 8,000' due south of Saidor, near where I had flown. The required reports were made to the CIL [the Army's Central Identification Laboratory] and soon I called to ask when they might be going to investigate the site. Fortunately, they were preparing for the recovery of another P-47, piloted by Lieutenant Wilfrid Desilets, that Hagen had located two years earlier. Their departure would be delayed due to a tsunami, resulting in a curtailed schedule. I was devastated when they advised me there might not be time to look at "my" P-47. I pleaded with strength that came from my soul.

The weather in the Finisterres made flying difficult, but after several attempts, the CIL team got into the site on October 6. I waited for the phone to ring until Friday, October 16, when I received word from Hagen that the team had identified two of the .50-caliber guns listed on the MACR. My first call was to the CIL for official confirmation. I asked if it meant I could tell my mother. "Yes," came the response. . . .

I flew to Hawaii on June 1 [1999] to escort my father home. I was told I'm the first family member ever to have escorted the repatriated remains of an Army serviceman. As the plane left Honolulu, a lifetime of tears burst forth. This was it, my father was no longer lost and alone in those mountains. He was with me, and I was taking him home. I had daydreamed about him teaching me to fly or taking me on a Sunday drive in the clouds. Now we were on a plane together—not as I would have wanted, but it was much more than I'd ever expected to have.

Mother was waiting at the airport in Madison, Wisconsin. As we embraced she said, "You did it, Patty, you brought him home." When we went to the cargo area to wait for the hearse, the handler said, "I'm an old Army man." We stood in silence as he saluted my father's casket. On June 5 a Funeral Mass was held at St. Raphael Cathedral, where my father had been baptized and served as an altar boy. The pallbearers were his childhood friends. Twelve boys had gone to war; only one had not come home.

FOR GENEVA SHELTON OF HAWTHORNE, California, the trauma of losing her brother in the war has not faded. He was in Belgium, advancing on Germany, in mid-December 1944.

So many of your words in the book reminded me of my brother, especially "D-Day" and the "Battle of the Bulge," as he was a part of both.

My brother, Ralph Stewart, was so very much like so many of your heroes—in his twenties and engaged to be married when war became the master of his life. He was a gentle, sensitive soul, with unbounded love for his mother and for our sister's little girl, who died after a brief illness at the tender age of five. I could never imagine him manning a machine gun. . . .

So many thoughts of my brother were aroused as I read your book, including some rather remarkable ones. First, to this day his Army Serial Number is imprinted on my mind—18035832—always ready for immediate recall. Then there was the time when I had an incredibly vivid dream: My sister and I were at a County Fair, where there was a closely-packed crowd of people. Some distance away in that crowd we saw our brother Ralph—the perfect likeness of him in his Army uniform, as in a photograph which I have. My sister and I were anxiously discussing how we were going to be able to tell our mother

that we had found Ralph, who after all
had not been a casualty of war! We
were eagerly working our way through
the mass of people so that he would not
disappear among them before we could
reach him. But, as seems to be the way
with dreams, just as we were getting
close enough to reach out to him, I
awoke from the dream. Then there was
a later time, about forty years after
Ralph's death, when I was the principal
of an elementary school. Each morning
I prepared an information bulletin to
post in the staff room. On two occasions that I remember, the date which I
typed was December 18, 1944—the
date on which my brother was killed in
battle. I was not consciously thinking of
him at the time; but that date, like that
Army Serial Number, was indelibly
printed on my mind. . . .

When my brother's remains arrived
for reburial in his hometown of Morton,
Texas, attached to the end of his casket
were his "dog tags"—18035832. . . .

I still have the flag which was draped
over my brother's coffin, and was placed

in my mother's hands at his reburial service on November 23, 1947.

FOR THOSE WHO SURVIVED, THE LOSS OF their buddies was as traumatic as the loss of a family member. Many had to ponder why they had lived, and then write to the families of those who did not. Lou Cocker Flowers of Virginia Beach, Virginia, sent a collection of letters written by her father, a Navy pilot.

> Perhaps you would be interested in my father's story. [He was] Lieut. (j.g.) Roland Matthew Cocker, U.S. Navy.
> On May 10, 1945, the PBM plane he piloted went down in the Pacific; nine of the twelve men on board perished. On only a few occasions did he tell the story in detail. . . . His personal account told the story of regaining consciousness and struggling to open the cockpit hatch; being injured and disoriented, underwater in the dark; holding his breath until he thought his lungs would burst; and being surrounded by fluorescent algae creating confusion as

to which surface was the ocean and which was the starlit sky. It was also clear that he had a spiritual moment that night that changed his life, but that went without much discussion as I believe it was intensely private to him.

The exchange of letters between my father and the crew's families is incredibly moving. They reveal the courtesy, civility, dignity and sacrificial spirit of the time.

My father lived to be an F.B.I. agent for 30 years, a devoted husband to my mother Annie Laurie for 53 years and a beloved father to my sister, brother and me. He died of cancer November 28, 1996.

This is Lieutenant Cocker's letter to the parents of a crew member:

It was 10 o'clock at night at ███* when the plane's right side burst into flames where there is a gas tank of several

* Censored by the military.

hundred gallons. (Investigations determined a leaking gas line.) The fire was impossible to extinguish and the plane rapidly filled with smoke, being at a low-bombing altitude our only chance was to land in the open sea. The night was extremely dark and the glare from the flames was partially blinding, the waves had a long rolling swell which culminated in extremely hazardous landing. The plane evidently broke in two about midships. After several violent attempts to land, everyone was knocked unconscious by the impact and water filled the plane immediately as it began to sink. The co-pilot was thrown through the windshield and was seriously injured, the bow gunner escaped through the hatch nearest him, and I as pilot narrowly escaped through the window. *Your son* was at his post performing his duties to the best of his ability and you may be assured that it was through no fault of any of the crew members that this incident occurred, and it was only a miracle that three of us got out of it. The area was combed thoroughly by air and by sea for several days but no signs were ever revealed of any other survivors.

It is you loved ones [who] must bear the brunt of war, so let us all pray and work together that there may be no more of this grievance. With heads high and shoulders square, you parents and wives are the truly unsung heroes of this war.

And here are four letters that Lieutenant Cocker received from crew members' families.

Dear Lieut. Cocker,

If you don't mind I would like to ask you a few questions. You may not be able to answer them all, but I would certainly appreciate it if you would answer all you can for me. There are so many unanswered questions running through my mind that it makes things worse. I don't know whether you are a married man or not, Lieutenant, but if you are you will understand my feelings I'm sure, and bear with me.

1. Was the Plane afire all over or just the engines?
2. Was Homer alright the last time you saw him?
3. Did you three survivors bail out or get out after the plane crashed?
4. Had the plane sunk or was it still afloat the last time you saw it?
5. Did you see Homer after the plane caught fire if so what was he doing?
6. They may not let you answer this, but was there any explosion before or after the crash?
7. Was the plane shot at, or bombed, or was the fire caused by the engine trouble?
8. Do you have any kind of proof that the other boys went down, any definite reason to believe they didn't get out too, or do you base your opinion on the fact that none of them have been found?

Answer my questions the best you can, please Lieutenant. They have been spinning around in my head unanswered so long, it's almost driven me crazy.

I can face whatever is to come, with the help of the Lord, Lieutenant Cocker, but I'm afraid I can't accept the opinion that Homer is dead, until there is some proof or time tells its own story. I have the faith you spoke of in your letter, but it's faith that somewhere, somehow, in the face of it all, God hasn't failed to answer my prayers and those of our babies.

I will appreciate anything you can tell me in regards to the answers to the questions.

Very sincerely,
Mrs. Homer Chancellor

Dear Lieutenant Cocker:

Your letter of June 10th has been received. Both Mr. Brill and I wish to express our sincere appreciation for your thoughtfulness in writing relative to our son Roland. It is gratifying to us to know that you considered him a personal friend and that his conduct and personality merited your kind words of commendation.

While we feel our loss very keenly we have the satisfaction of knowing that he was in the branch of service he liked most. We can only hope that his sacrifice and that of his comrades will hasten the coming of victory and bring lasting peace.

Very sincerely yours,
Mrs. Roland C. Brill

My Dear Lieut:

We thank you for the very sincere letter you have sent us at a time like this. The suspense was most distressing. We are thankful that Gordon was associated with a Christian pilot such as you have indicated to us that you are. We also appreciate your thoughtfulness in sending us the picture and memorial program and other details you were allowed to give us at this time.

If you wish we would appreciate corresponding with you from time to time, Mrs. Guether would like to write to the remainder of the crew also, since she can no longer write to Gordon we would like to have the present as well as the home addresses of all of you men.

I believe that this would encourage her quite much. I know she would be happy to write to all of you.

If at any time day or night you should be in Chicago or vicinity you are most cordially invited to call and stay with us.

Sincerely yours,

Mr. & Mrs. C. E. Guether

Lieut. Roland M. Cocker,

Dear Friend.

I thank you very much for letting me hear from you, and giving me as much information as you could about my boy Wiley Ross Hanson . . . that is missing in the accident at sea.

I hope that you and the other two survivors will be lucky enough that you will not have to go through with such awful experience again, and will live to get back, and when you get back don't forget to write to me and give us the full details of the accident.

You are all remembered in our Prayers.

Very truly yours.

Mr. & Mrs. J. P. Hanson

SOME FAMILIES HAVE THE COMFORT OF knowing their loved one died a hero. Shirley Colgan Goodwyne of Jacksonville, Florida, describes her brother William Winfield Colgan, a medic with the Marines. He died in one of the most ferocious battles of the war, on the island of Peleliu, where the Japanese were entrenched in deep caves on hostile terrain. William was awarded the Navy Cross, one of that service's highest decorations, for his bravery.

The whole family was affected by my brother's death and my mother got real sick and almost gave up on living. After a talk with her brother, she realized she had eight other children to raise and got on with the task. Very rarely, if ever, did we speak about William, because of the hurt it was to all of us.

During the fifty-year reunion of WWII, I met some men that did not know my brother, but who had served on Peleliu, the battle my brother was killed in. . . .

William was four months shy of his 21st birthday, but he lived a thoughtful, good clean life. . . .

It says in his yearbook, "Ambition— To be an Admiral in the U.S. Navy." He did not make admiral, but his name will always be a part of naval history, as an enlisted man who received the Navy Cross for extraordinary heroism. . . .

We now speak of William often, and every now and then, someone remembers a story that brings it back to us. His nephew Russell William Allen, who was born years after his uncle's death, has a web page dedicated to the memory of his uncle. The U.R.L. is http://www.imswebs.com/russallen~peleliu—take a look at it, he did a great job.

Shirley also enclosed a letter her brother wrote to his parents in the event something happened to him.

Dear Mom + Dad,

As you know I had 10 thousand dollars insurance and there is something I want you to do if you should have to collect. I want for you to buy a house, out near the park, you can pay it off on the F.H.A. plan, the insurance will be paid off at the rate of about 50 a month + I think the F.H.A. is on the plan of paying off a house at the rate of 30 or 40 dollars a month.

If you can, also send Edith to college when she gets old enough, don't do like you let me do get by without studying, make her. She'll probably be as smart as Dolly, it's [too] bad she couldn't have gone to college as she really deserved to go. Well there isn't much more a fellow can say, I just hope Dolly doesn't ever have to give you this letter. Love to you all.

Your Loving Son
William

P.S. Make Elwood save his money + try to get him to go to college. It really pays, get him interested in aviation or television that what is really going to pay off in the future.

THE SECRETARY OF THE NAVY
WASHINGTON

The President of the United States takes pride in presenting the NAVY CROSS posthumously to

WILLIAM WINFIELD COLGAN
PHARMACIST'S MATE SECOND CLASS
UNITED STATES NAVAL RESERVE

for service as set forth in the following

CITATION:

"For extraordinary heroism while serving with the Third Battalion, Seventh Marines, First Marine Division, Fleet Marine Force, during action against enemy Japanese Forces at Peleliu, Palau Islands, on October 4, 1944. Realizing that many wounded men were pinned down by intense enemy machine-gun, rifle and mortar fire, COLGAN unhesitatingly proceeded far in front of his own lines in order to administer first aid to the casualties. When our troops were forced to withdraw from untenable positions, he courageously exposed himself to a withering barrage from Japanese guns and directed the men to take cover until a protective smoke screen could be lowered, then skillfully supervised evacuation of the wounded until he was fatally struck down by Japanese fire. COLGAN's daring initiative and great personal valor in the face of grave peril were in keeping with the highest traditions of the United States Naval Service. He gallantly gave his life for his country."

For the President,

James Forrestal

Secretary of the Navy

CHARLES J. LEONARD, JR., WAS A MARINE rifleman on Okinawa in 1945. He now lives in Danville, California, but he has a special connection to the American cemetery called the Punchbowl, above Pearl Harbor in Hawaii.

I enlisted in the Marines on "Armistice" Day, 1944. I trained at San Diego and Camp Pendleton. I shipped out with 5000 other 17 and 18 year old Marines the day after President (*our President*) Roosevelt died. We went to Guam for a few weeks as the advance party for the thousands of Marines who would be needed for the invasion of Japan. However, a sudden need for Marines developed in early May 1945 because of the fierce fighting on Okinawa. 2,500 of us were placed aboard an APA (the *Clinton*) and 5 days later we were off Okinawa, dodging kamikazes. . . .

We unloaded into the mud and trudged up to the front lines, which resembled WWI. The Japanese had 70 miles of tunnels and the *entire Japanese*

174 / TOM BROKAW

32nd Army (116,000 Japanese soldiers) was underground. We had to come at them out in the open and we paid the price. My Battalion (2nd Bt. 1st Regt) had landed on Okinawa with 32 officers and 869 men. When the battle ended 82 days later, 32 officers and 872 men had been *killed or wounded.* These figures don't include the hundreds of Marines who were disabled by dysentery and malaria or had their senses knocked out of them by the heaviest use of artillery and mortars by the Japanese anywhere in the Pacific. I was wounded June 12, 1945.

The war ended on Aug. 15 just as my hospital ship, the USS *Repose,* was entering San Francisco Bay.

I shall never forget the dozens of buddies who fell beside me. Every Memorial Day I become very emotional. Those of us who survived were so very lucky and we are thankful.

The following piece, also by Charles Leonard, appeared in the *Contra Costa Times.*

A Marine Buddy Cheats Death Once— but Not Twice

Eighteen-year-old private Wayne L. Lyons was my buddy. During World War II we served together in the Second Battalion, First Regiment, First Marine Division. I was a bazooka rifleman in F Company and Wayne was a rifleman in G Company.

Late in the afternoon of June 9, 1945, while Second Battalion was engaged in heavy fighting on the island of Okinawa, Wayne's platoon was caught out in the open while advancing. Eight Marines, including the commanding officer, were killed. Six were disabled by wounds and Wayne was slightly scratched in the hand by a bullet. The Japanese poured rifle fire into the bodies, so Wayne crawled underneath his dead friend, Bill Pierce. Pierce's body protected him until several of us could get to him after darkness set in. Most of the wounded were dead, but Wayne had survived.

When we got back to safety, Wayne was emotionally distraught. I held him for several minutes until he got control and then we shook hands and he went back to G Company, his uniform dark red with Pierce's blood.

Two days later, I was wounded and evacuated to the United States. Four days later, while assaulting a heavily protected ridge, a Japanese shell hit my friend, Wayne, and blew him to pieces. The shell was seen to explode where he lay, so he was listed as missing in action at the Punchbowl Cemetery above Pearl Harbor in Honolulu.

In 1985 my wife, Donna, and I returned to Okinawa and left a small memorial marker and a flag where Wayne died.

The memory of my good friend Wayne bravely returning to his company and thence to his death will live with me forever.

IN *THE GREATEST GENERATION* I WROTE about Mary Louise Roberts, an Army nurse who was the first woman to receive the Silver Star, for her courageous conduct while her surgical tent was being shelled on Anzio. I described how six nurses had been killed at Anzio. That caught the attention of Nancy Keister of South Yarmouth, Massachusetts, and brought back memories of one of those women.

In 1940, ten days after my son was born in Columbia Presbyterian Hospital in New York City, I was diagnosed as having scarlet fever and was taken away to Willard Parker Hospital for Contagious Diseases on the Lower East Side. I was not brave like the people in your book and felt very scared and disheartened at being separated from my husband and baby. This quarantine was to last three weeks. My husband was able to get one of the two private nurses available for this duty. Her name was Blanche Sigman. Without her loving care, I would have been a sad case.

When I returned home to my new baby and family, I kept in close contact with Blanche. She planned to go into the army and hoped to become a doctor when the war was over. Over the next few years we corresponded, and I sent packages and letters to her as she traveled through Africa and on to Italy. One day my letter was returned, marked "Deceased." As I did not know her stepmother in Ohio, I had no idea what had happened.

I learned something of Blanche when my brother, W. O. Cromwell, served in the Philippines, where he married an army nurse, Capt. Sarah Hale, sometime in the late 40's. When they came back to the U.S., I told Sarah about Blanche, saying I realized it was very iffy, but could she tell me anything about her. As it happened, she could. She said Blanche had been killed in Anzio when the Germans shelled the hospital. There was also a cargo ship, I think, named after her and I was able to spot it in the shipping news when it was in the port of New York.

And there my story of Blanche ended until today, when I got to the chapter

"Women in Uniform and Out," where I read, "Ellen Ainsworth, killed by German artillery shell—one of six nurses to die at Anzio"—and my dear Blanche, also, one of them. Now, so many years later, at 81 years of age, I am able to shed tears in her dear memory.

AFTER BEING FIRED BY PRESIDENT HARRY Truman in April 1951, General Douglas MacArthur gave a speech before Congress in which he said, famously, "Old soldiers never die, they just fade away." Sadly, the veterans of World War II are now fading away at the rate of thirty thousand a month.

Mary Griffiths was married to an old soldier, a career Army officer, and they were retired in Columbia, South Carolina, when he died.

Last night my husband died as I held him in my arms, and I told him, "I love you, and go on home soldier, your mom and dad are waiting on you, give our Fay a kiss—wait for me. I will join you soon, wait for me"—with that, 2 big tears rolled down his cheeks (he hadn't opened his eyes for 2 days)—but I knew then he heard me—he took his last breath and left me.

Tomorrow I pick up his remains, and will bring him home for the last time, and take him to Beaufort, South Carolina, National Cemetery for burial. It was his wish and mine to be cremated, and be buried. He did not want any service; this is my wish too. . . .

Like so many [of those whose] personal accounts I have read in your book—he too had to be "pulled out" to talk about his experiences. He chose Army as a career—when I said goodbye to him in 1941—I did not see him for 3 years & 8 months, his war was [the] Pacific War, then he hit the Korean War again for 2 years—he wears "9 battle stripes" on his sleeve and "combat infantry badge, with a silver star"—these are the only decorations that really counted to him, that he prized. He received numerous other decorations though. . . .

The Army was our life, for 24 years. I loved every minute of it *except* the separation for wars.

I always tried to represent my husband, the Army, and the U. States honorably, wherever we were stationed.

I guess the happiest time in his life [was] when he returned to Ohio, and his 148th Regimental reunion, after 40 years or so, and he was re-united with the men that served under him [when he was] a Captain in World War II for 3 years and 8 months. . . .

Putting this down has given me much comfort to talk to you tonight.

MARTHA TILLER OF RICHMOND, VIRGINIA, grew up in a hurry when war broke out.

I was a sophomore in college when Pearl Harbor was attacked, so my life went from carefree—praying not to die before the next fraternity dance—to praying for all the boys I knew to come home safely. My husband and his brother were killed within six months of each other, and my favorite co-cheerleader died at Guadalcanal.

Martha was attending Sophie Newcomb College in New Orleans when she met George Tompkins, a student at Tulane. He was commissioned a second lieutenant in the Army Air Corps. They had one son, George Junior, before her husband was killed in action.

I was remarried about eight years after he was killed. I was engaged a couple of times and backed off. I was crazy about my husband. . . . It takes a long time. We had one son . . . and he is a pilot just like his father. Genes are so power-ful. His father saw him just one time, and then went overseas. And then he was killed when [the child] was six months old. My son is a pilot just like he was, and he loves fast cars just like he did, and he even has the same exact signature. . . .

My father-in-law was a West Point graduate, in Eisenhower's class, and had a great deal to do in the war. They had three sons and lost two of them within six months of each other. . . . The third was a Marine, and they could have requested his return as the only surviving child of the family. But he pleaded not to be sent back home; he wanted to fight more than ever. He said that with his two brothers being killed, he wanted to fight for them. And he made it home safely, so that turned out all right.

OF ALL THOSE IN UNIFORM DURING World War II, only a fraction were directly exposed to enemy fire. The ratio of men in infantry divisions to those in backup positions was one to four. One of those behind the lines was Roger Newburger of White Plains, New York, who was with the Army Corps of Engineers during World War II.

I put in my time (4 years & 6 days) in World War 2. But my Corps of Engineers outfit was in battle only once and very wisely I was left behind on Oahu with six enlisted men with the company's gear that wasn't carted into the front lines.

I say "wisely" because a warrior I am not and never was. I'm sure that if I had been sent into battle I would have tried to do whatever I was told or supposed to do, but I think the guys would have been safer without me firing anywhere near them.

In fact, I also would have been safer. . . .

Saving Private Ryan is the only movie I didn't see with my wife of 48 years. I walked out of the theater, walked slowly to my car, got in and sat for about a half-hour, with one sob and a few tears rolling down my cheeks. Afterwards, I decided I was thus affected because of what the real warriors went through.

The movie's premise is that Ryan's three brothers have been killed in action and he must be pulled off the front lines before he's lost as well. In fact, many families lost more than one son. Barbara Peterson of River Vale, New Jersey, is the great-granddaughter of a woman who lost two sons. She wrote about how her family dealt with the loss of her grandfather and great-uncle, both killed in Europe.

My grandfather John W. Rockwell and his only brother, Malcolm H. Rockwell, were killed in 1944, World War II, Europe. Within two months, my great-grandmother lost her only two sons and my mother, at age three, lost her father and her uncle. To this day, my mother swears she can remember the Western Union knock on the door that changed her life forever.

My grandmother never remarried and, to my knowledge, never even dated another man after the loss of her husband. Shortly after John's death in October 1944, Malcolm wrote my grandmother to share his sorrow about the loss of his brother, her beloved husband. In his letter, Malcolm hoped that the war would soon end so as "to spare some other family the grief that is ours." That was the last time my grandmother heard from him. He was killed in the Battle of the Bulge, December 1944.

Both men are buried overseas, my grandfather at the American Military Cemetery, Normandy, France, and Uncle Mac at Henri-Chapelle Cemetery, Belgium. I had the honor of being the first family member to visit my grandfather's grave, in the fall of 1997. As you know, words cannot describe the feeling of standing on the grounds of this magnificent cemetery overlooking Omaha Beach.

ELEANOR FOSTER OF BELLEVUE, MICHIgan, wrote about the pain of losing her first husband, Lawrence "Danny" Danforth, who was killed in action in Sicily in 1943.

I am 83 years old—you can say a victim of World War II. No, I was not in actual combat, but my losses are real.

It is difficult to explain the emptiness I am experiencing today. First for having lost my husband *and* to have lost the family we were to have had. It isn't because I want to lean on children; instead, it is missing the joys of seeing new families created, the sharing of family memories, the sharing of experiences and love with grandchildren, the knowledge that children are there to give guidance and support as needs arise with the aging process. All of this was sacrificed!

Danny, my husband, and I met when I was teaching in Janesville, Wisconsin. Danny was with Chevrolet Motors in Janesville, building a future with the industry. We were engaged—I had my ring—and then the draft came along. In Janesville anyone who was married was automatically exempted from the draft. Marriages occurred at an accelerated rate! With due consideration, Danny and I decided that we had an obligation to answer the need for trained men for our country and wanted to put off our wedding plans until after he had fulfilled his 2-year draft call. Drafted the summer of 1941, completed Officer Training, 2nd Lt., in 1942. I had taken a job with the University of Illinois Extension Service as Home Adviser in Belvedere, Illinois. The husband of the secretary for the Extension Service was in the regular army, Captain Cleveland. [The secretary] was concerned about our situation and, with the increased seriousness of the war, we did decide to be married in the fall of 1942. Danny was killed in action in Sicily in July 1943. I had to pull my life together and relocate in the business world. . . . Although I married many years later, a family was not in my future. Danny and I gave up being married and having a family to answer the draft . . . this we did with, as you said, a purpose and with modesty!

VINCENT DE VITTO OF LAKE RONKONKOMA, New York, is one of five sons of Raffaele and Luigia De Vitto, first-generation immigrants from Italy. All five of the De Vitto boys served during World War II; one of them, Liberty, was killed in France. Vincent De Vitto sent a copy of the letter that his sister Mary wrote to the brothers to break the news of Liberty's death.

Dear Boys,

I've put off writing to you for a few days now, hoping that in time I could soften the blow that I must give you. You already know that Lib was wounded in France, and perhaps you have suspected that the final results would not be pleasant.

Saturday, September 16, we received another telegram from the war department stating that Lib had died from wounds received. He was wounded on the 22nd of August and he died August 24, in France.

I know this news must be pretty horrible for you boys to take, for it hasn't been easy for us. We were so sick over it that I neglected to write to you before. I only hope that you boys can take it as well as Lib took Dad's death. Mom has been very worried about you boys not being able to take it, and it would be a consolation to her if all of you would write and assure her that you are all making the best of it. As for me, I realize how this news is going to affect you so please for Mom's sake keep well. If you'll just remember that it's God's will that these things happen. It isn't too much of a comfort, I know, but it's the only one I can give you.

You all know how Lib was well known and liked for his sincerity. Everyone feels very sad about his passing on like that.

Please be brave about this and remember to write Mom. Your letters mean as much to her as to me. I know I can depend on you.

Love, Mary

Vincent named one of his sons after Liberty and the boy grew up to be a drummer in Billy Joel's band. Vincent wrote, "On one of his world tours Billy introduced . . . Liberty, named after my brother who lost his life in action on the Brest peninsula. He told the audience that his drummer's father had helped liberate Bastogne with the 101st. Liberty received a standing ovation."

Vincent lost a brother but he said he received from the service "the deep satisfaction . . . that I joined the ranks of many before me in serving my country, and the loyalty and commitment, discipline and sacrifices that I observed and experienced will never leave my memories. I thank God for my good fortune and pray that no generation will face war again."

IV

FAITH

Chaplain Sam Neel. After he was released from a German POW camp, Neel carried this photograph in his wallet for more than fifty years.

Gino Merli, September 5, 1944, in Sars-la-Bruyère, Belgium, where he earned the Congressional Medal of Honor.

IXB 23630

———————— • ————————

Were members of the Greatest Generation more spiritual or religiously faithful than their offspring or succeeding generations? Spirituality is difficult to quantify, but it's clear from the letters I received, and from anecdotal and other evidence from organized religions, that faith and religious belief were widely and openly embraced.

Certainly the combat veterans with whom I spoke were for the most part men who could testify to the truth of the saying that there are no atheists in foxholes. Philip L. Cochran of Maple City, Michigan, was not a chaplain; he was a combat Marine. But his description of what happened one night typifies what many veterans experienced.

One night, on Guadalcanal, while leading a reconnaissance patrol, we were pinned down by sniper fire and in the ensuing melee, I was all alone, out in the middle of the jungle, not having the vaguest idea of my location. . . . I have never been so scared, but you know what, I discovered the power of prayer at that moment, a power I never had to call upon before, but a power for which I had occasion to be grateful many times during the war, a power I have relied upon throughout my life since then.

There are countless other stories of the place of faith in the lives of the men on the front lines and of their families and friends who were praying daily for their well-being. It is not surprising that after *The Greatest Generation* was published I heard from former military chaplains and their admirers, gently suggesting I should have included a tribute to their role.

They're right, of course.

Lenora F. Clark of Houston, Texas, was one of those who wrote; her husband, Lamar, was a chaplain assigned to the Pacific theater.

These persons were not conscripted, but all were volunteers. In most cases they were a little older than the average soldier because the qualifications were so high . . . all were required to have the amount of education which their denomination demanded before ordination, and ordination and recommendation were prerequisite to being accepted. Their age, however, did not prevent them going through the same hardships as the younger soldiers *unarmed.* . . . I know all of this by my personal contact with a chaplain before he entered the military and during the time he spent in actual combat with an infantry unit and recorded in letters written every day he was overseas (except when cut off behind enemy lines and unable to write). I have all these personal letters now copied and bound into five books. They tell of the dangers he faced, the men he buried, the letters he wrote to wives, or parents, or children, or sisters, or friends to try to explain what had happened to their loved one who died fighting for freedom.

Not only did these men live in foxholes, survive behind the enemy lines,
starve along with all the others when
there was no food, or no fresh meat or
vegetables or fruit for weeks and sometimes months on end, but they gave
encouragement to those who were
fighting and being wounded and, in
some cases, [were] wounded themselves. The particular chaplain whom I
knew and from whom I received hundreds of letters, some written on a typewriter when one was available in a
tent-office, but most of them in long-
hand, came home with a Purple Heart,
a Bronze Star with several clusters, and
a Presidential Citation earned in his
first combat mission on Leyte.

And [the chaplains] did not just fade
away into the background at home. They
became pastors, church administrators,
teachers of theology, hospital chaplains
and many other kinds of leaders, most of
whom never earned large salaries.

Mrs. Clark elaborated on her life with her
husband.

We met the first day of college in freshman English class and were attracted to each other. Very soon we were deeply in love—love that lasted the rest of our lives. We were married on April 26, 1936, and six years later, on that date, he reported to the Army in Indianapolis. When war was declared, he felt compelled to volunteer to help to pay for our freedom and all the good things that had come to us because of the sacrifice of others. I was not all that enthusiastic, because I had two small children and no home. But he felt so strongly, I could not prevail. After two years of training with a newly organized division, he asked for and got an overseas assignment and on April 26, 1944, he sailed for the South Pacific, going first to New Caledonia and then to New Guinea where he spent several months with an ordnance battalion where he built a chapel out of native materials using native labor. But that did not satisfy him. Again, he asked for combat duty. As the letters will indicate, he was assigned to a division that made the initial landing on the Philippines.

Chaplain Clark's letters home are reminders of the frontline perils of trying to serve God and combat infantrymen simultaneously.

26 October 1944

My Darling Lenora Fay,

I did not write in the mountains because the picture was such that I would not have wanted you to know what it was. I'll say this: I am sure that the papers were full of the 2nd Bn. [Battalion] 19th Regt. Things were bad, but I knew it would come out to you. I don't want to write this but it will get in the paper sooner or later through the public relations officer. I was wounded but only slightly. For polite company it was on the posterior. Yes, I got hit on the side of the "butt." . . . It was glancing and caused only a slight wound. It went through my jacket and pants and broke the skin. It only bled a little.

I am truly a veteran now. I have been through everything, but am more convinced than ever of Divine Protection. . . . Please have faith in me and our prayers to put God's love around me.

27 October 1944

Darling, I am afraid that you will feel that I have not been fair so I'll give this brief resume since I left. . . .

We had a very rough and dangerous time in the mountains with little food or anything else. Sometime I'll tell you more.

I am safe and whole and am coming back to you as I promised. I never did needlessly expose myself [to danger], and I won't.

The men are in good shape and their spirit is good. I am glad of that.

28 October 1944

My beautiful love, I love you so much. You and our darling babies are my whole life. Through you, God has taught and is teaching me what He wants me to know. I can never be grateful enough for you all. Never will I be able to pay for the blessings that are mine. It is rough here, and I'll see more, but all of that will not pay for you all. You all are worth all of this and more too. You know that all of this comes from the depth of my very being. I want you to know what you all mean to me and this knowledge will bring me back to you.

SAM NEEL, JR., OF BRADENTON, FLORIDA, served as an Army chaplain with the 106th Infantry Division. He spent Christmas Eve 1944 as a German POW. His wife, Eleanor, sent the following letter:

He is now 85 years old and frail. His hand is unsteady, thus I am writing for him. . . . I was not a part of Sam's life during those years. We have been married since 1971, after we both were widowed. I tell everyone that Sam's war stories do indeed show how brave he is—but the bravest thing he ever did was marry me, a widow with 6 young children.

The letter Neel dictated to his wife describes the events leading up to his capture.

Shortly after dawn there was an artillery barrage such as I have never heard before or since. It was the beginning of the Battle of the Bulge. The Germans decided to make their break-through by hitting two regiments of our division and one regiment of the 28th Division with 12 divisions of tanks and infantry. Our regiment managed to hold its position, but the Germans broke through north of us and south of us, and they just kept on going towards Belgium and France. The last communication we received was to hold our position as long as we could. After 1½ days, a runner named Lt. Starr from headquarters finally got through to us and told us to pull out and go mount an attack on Schoenberg, which was 15 miles behind us. There was more than a foot of snow on the ground. In fact, it was a severe winter and it was almost 3 months later before we ever saw the ground again. The German meteorologist had chosen wisely and there was a low overcast for almost a week. No American planes had been able to fly supplies to us. We were out of food and ammunition. Lt. Starr told me that Schoenberg was defended by a division of tanks. I decided that if we reached Schoenberg and launched an attack against the tanks with bayonets, I was going to try to find some troops near the rear to minister to.

The next 24 hours were hell. We were moving across hills and valleys, but the German tanks and artillery kept firing at us and finally we ended up on Dec. 19th on a flat-top hill completely surrounded. There were dead and wounded lying everywhere and our colonel decided to surrender. It was early afternoon and the Germans permitted me to take 25 men with picks and shovels and an armed guard. We buried American dead until dark.

At Gerolstein, the Germans herded us onto the railroad platform where we were to be loaded onto boxcars. I was walking back and forth inquiring about friends as to whether they were alive or dead. Somebody introduced me to a Dr. Sutherland from another outfit. Dr. Sutherland—Chaplain Neel. We talked rather formally for a couple of minutes and then I turned and started on. Evidently there is a characteristic way that I carry one arm because Doc took one look at the way I walked and he yelled, "Hey, are you Sam Neel?" I turned and took another look at him and said, "Yes, are you Josh Sutherland?" We had been classmates for three years in college. We were so bearded and haggard that we didn't recognize each other from the front, but he recognized my back.

The Germans gave us a little food and water and then we were piled into the old "40 and 8" boxcars of World War

I vintage. The cars were supposed to carry 40 men and 8 horses. Evidently they had the horses on before us, because we were crowded in on 6 inches of horse manure. There were so many of us that no one could lie down. We all had to sit up.

They kept us in the cars like animals for 3½ days. We weren't permitted to get out and there was no food or water. I began to wonder if the Germans were systematically torturing us.

Finally, near nightfall on December 23rd, our train stopped in the railroad yard of Limberg, Germany. We were permitted out of the cars for a few minutes; then they gave us a little food and water. Each of us had a small piece of black bread which was so coarse it looked like it was made out of sawdust. They also gave us a spoonful of molasses each. Doc Buxton, who was sitting next to me, had let them use his helmet to bring our molasses in, and they had given him a spoon to dish it out. Before we ate they asked me to give a prayer of thanksgiving for the food. Just as I was finishing the prayer, the air raid siren in Limberg sounded and a host of RAF bombers came flying over. Our railroad yard was the target for the night. As we heard the first bomb swish in the air, one man yelled, "Watch out men, here come the bombs, put on your steel helmets." So, Doc Buxton threw on his helmet and molasses went all over him. It was a nerve-racking ordeal but after it was over we had a good laugh as we helped Doc lick his way out.

The next morning when we looked out there was one crater within 30 yards of our car. When that one hit, we must have had the feeling that you have just before you go off into eternity. We also saw dead Americans lying all over the railroad yard. These were the men who had broken out of their cars in trying to run away from the bombs.

As the morning moved along, the men still alive sat in their cars and the train wasn't moving. You could feel the tension mounting because each of us was thinking, "If this train doesn't move, we will still be sitting here tonight and the bombers will come again." Finally, an interpreter in our car who could speak German talked to one of the guards. He suggested that the Germans permit me, the chaplain, to go from car to car and try to quiet the men. To our surprise, the guard consented.

As I went from car to car, I reminded the men that it was Dec. 24th, Christmas Eve. I suggested that they go, in their hearts and minds, back to their homes where their families were gathered around the Christmas trees, and that they have a Christmas service of some kind in each car.

When I got back to our car, darkness had fallen. I recited to our men the Christmas story from Matthew which begins, "Now when Jesus was born in Bethlehem of Judea, in the days of Herod the King..." Then I gave a Christmas prayer and we began to sing Christmas carols. When we sang "Silent

Night, Holy Night," which is a German carol of course, our guard knocked on the side of the car. Through our interpreter he asked us to sing the carol again. He did not recognize the English words, but he recognized the tune. As we sang I could see the men beginning to relax. Then, in conclusion, one man with a beautiful voice sang Brahms's Lullaby. We began drifting off to sleep. Then suddenly, our car gave a jolt and the train began to move. A great shout of joy went up from all of us, because we were moving out of that dreadful railroad yard. It was the best Christmas present any of us had ever had.

The prison camp itself was quite an ordeal. They didn't have room for us at permanent American camps, so we were taken to a prison camp for the Russians.

It was a very challenging experience for me. The first Sunday we had worship service. The men crowded into barracks and stood the entire time. I was up on a small platform and beside me was a can with a pussy-willow in it which someone had found to use as a worship center. As I looked out I could see the men's eyes saying, "You talked a lot about religion back in the States, but what can it do for men who are faced with being cold and hungry day after day, week after week?" I couldn't have met the challenge on my own, but I had an old battered New Testament which I had managed to keep each time we were searched by the Germans. That week I had run across a passage in Philippians. I reminded the men that Paul wrote this letter when he was a prisoner and was being persecuted. Then I read Philippians, the 4th chapter, the 11th through the 13th verses: "I have learned, in whatsoever state I am, therewith to be content. I know both how to be abused and how to abound. Everywhere and in all things I am instructed both to be full and to be hungry, both to abound and to suffer need, I can do all things through Christ who strengtheneth me." I didn't need to preach, the Scripture preached for me. And that's how it was Sunday after Sunday.

JOHN CRAVEN OF MCLEAN, VIRGINIA, WAS A
military chaplain in four campaigns during
World War II and three during the Korean
War. His story came to us from an April 6,
1995, article in the *Religious Herald,* the Virginia Baptists' weekly. The author is Pam
Parry.

Traumatized by mortar fire, the young
Marine huddled outside a military hospital, his body trembling, clenched into
a fetal position. "John the Baptist" took
his hand and began to pray, "Our Father
which art in heaven, hallowed be thy
name." The trembling continued. "Thy
kingdom come. Thy will be done on
earth, as it is in heaven."

In a moment, the Marine composed
himself enough to join the chaplain:
"Give us this day our daily bread. And
forgive us our debts, as we forgive our
debtors."

As they finished the Lord's Prayer the
soldier began to relax and the shaking
subsided. The most effective antidote
for shell shock is the Lord's Prayer, says
Chaplain John Craven of McLean, who

lived that dramatic scene numerous times during seven combat campaigns spanning more than 30 years of military service. Now retired from active duty, Craven, 79, is a chaplain at Vinson Hall Navy–Marine Corps Officers Retirement Residence in McLean.

Craven, a Southern Baptist, is thought to have seen more combat than any living chaplain. He participated in four campaigns during World War II, including the one at Iwo Jima, and three during the Korean War. On the 50th anniversary of the Iwo Jima campaign, Craven reflected on his participation in the historic battle. Craven, known affectionately as John the Baptist by the Fourth Marine Division, ministered to hundreds of wounded, dying and scared men. "I tried to visit the troops as often as I could to encourage them, talk to them," he said. For the most part the chaplain's role was helping to tend to the wounded, he added.

Often, all that Craven could do for the [Iwo Jima] wounded was to take some moistened gauze and wipe the volcanic ash from their eyes. . . .

Craven, a member of McLean Baptist Church, also baptized four men during his five weeks at Iwo Jima. Those men accepted Christ on the boat before they landed. To witness such new birth amid the death and devastation of attack was miraculous, he recalls. Five decades later, he returned to that island in the Pacific to participate in the dedication of a monument to the casualties on both sides. The Japanese and American veterans sat on opposite sides of the monument. After leading a prayer, Craven and a former Japanese captain who had become a Buddhist priest embraced, setting an example for the men. Later, Craven wrote: "Before leaving the beach and the spot where our command post had been, I photographed a small, green plant with a small, red bloom. To me, it represented the hopes and dreams for peace rising out of the blood-soaked sands of Iwo Jima. . . ."

One of Craven's many lasting memories of World War II is the time he shared a fox-hole on Iwo Jima with a Catholic chaplain, Henry Druffel. As Craven recalled in a telephone conversation more than fifty years later, that experience shared by two men representing different expressions of Christian faith linked them forever. In a letter, Craven reaffirmed his impression.

> We were both assigned to the 14th Marine Regiment, and we had about 3000 men. It was an impossible situation. The Army had four chaplains with each regiment. But with the Marines, the Navy provided just one Catholic and one Protestant chaplain per regiment. . . .
> I tried to visit the troops, the men, as often as I could. We had five battalions, so that took quite some time. I spent quite a lot of time at the aid station, where the wounded were being brought in. . . . Iwo Jima was a difficult situation from beginning to end.
> I landed at about five o'clock on D-Day, and it was two days later that we

fixed our foxhole together. It was a pretty good foxhole. The volcanic ash at Iwo Jima wasn't solid ground, it was easy to give way. It was all volcanic ash, so it wasn't easy to walk in. The two of us managed to get part of a Japanese airplane that had been shot down—part of the fuselage of the wreckage. So we put that over the top of the foxhole and put some sand on top of that. It worked fine. . . . We were in there during fire, but then we looked up at the jagged pieces of this fuselage above us that were shot up, and we thought that if we were hit, we'd get more damage from the fuselage than the enemy shell. . . . So we flipped the fuselage over and started enlarging the foxhole. But while we were digging, the Japanese opened up with firing right on us. So we'd dig a while and then duck down in the hole because they were firing over our heads. But when we were down, Chaplain Druffel looked at me and said, "This sure gives you an incentive to dig, don't it?" I'll always remember that! So we finished it, and got a piece of lumber from the beach and fixed up a pretty good foxhole. Just the two of us . . .

You always have some fear, though of course I'd been through three campaigns before that . . . so I was pretty well ready for combat. . . . But it was my first time in the foxhole with another chaplain. We were together about 45 days . . . we coordinated and knew what the other was doing, in lining up services and where we were going to be during the day. . . . And when we got back to Maui, we saw each other every day . . . but then I'd been overseas 18 months so I came home. . . . After the war, the Marines transferred me to Norfolk to serve on amphibious ships. I was an enlisted Marine in the 1930s, so I liked to serve with Marines. . . . And after Druffel got out he went to Indiana to his order and he taught school. He didn't have a regular church—he worked in this Catholic community as a priest.

He was a really great guy . . . really wonderful. We communicated about once a year. He came to stay with us once at our home. But he's been dead at least 10 years now. He had a good sense of humor, but was a very pleasant, devoted priest . . . he was out to serve the men and help them and minister to them, in every way he could. A great individual.

Henry Druffel wrote to Chaplain Craven on June 29, 1953, right after the Korean War.

Chaplain John H. Craven, USN
Arlington, Virginia

Dear Chaplain,
   Hi! John. Sure good to hear from YOU again. Wish I could attend the Reunion of the old 4th Division (I still wear its shoulder patch on my coat lapel and tell the kids it stands for the 4th Commandment) in Washington, DC, next week but on Monday I'm embarking for the other Washington on the other end of the country, namely, Washington State which is my original home.

Greetings and best regards to your wife and family whom I met out in California and have not forgotten. I'll be thinking about you all next week while traveling westward. The thought of you will be good company on a long lonesome train ride. Have a good time and tell all our old friends you see I haven't forgotten them.

Thanks a lot for writing and if we don't have the pleasure of meeting again here in this world I shall continue to hope and pray that we meet where we both thought we might meet while we were in that "super-foxhole" together out there on Iwo Jima some eight and a half years ago now.

God bless you always.

Your old teammate on "Maui no ka oi!"

RABBI JUDAH NADICH WAS THE FIRST JEWISH chaplain to serve in the European theater. He was summoned on the orders of General Dwight Eisenhower after a Jewish soldier was killed in a training accident and there was a dispute over whether he would be buried in a Jewish cemetery, as the local rabbi in Belfast urged, or in a military cemetery. Nadich became an important adviser to Eisenhower when the concentration camps were liberated. The camps led him to question his faith in God, but eventually he became one of New York City's most important spiritual leaders as rabbi of the Park Avenue Synagogue for thirty years.

I enlisted immediately after Pearl Harbor. At that time, I was a rabbi in Chicago, and I thought, if a rabbi should not be in the war, then who should? We had been reading in the press about what had been happening to the Jews. Of course, compared to what happened to them later, what happened in the beginning was very little. But still, it was very offensive that the windows of Jews were being smashed, and they were boycotted, and things like that. After I enlisted, I was ordered to Fort Bragg, North Carolina, where I served as the Jewish chaplain for the troops there. We had over 100,000 troops at Fort Bragg, including the 101st Airborne. . . .

I was sent from Fort Bragg to Brooklyn, New York, and after a brief wait at Fort Hamilton in Brooklyn, I was put aboard a Dutch freighter with about 14 or 15 officers. Three days out from England, we were attacked by German submarines. We lost three ships, but we were some 50 ships altogether. It wasn't very pleasant, especially when we would gather in a little room on the ship and listen to the radio. We could hear the German radio too, and we heard a woman, whoever she was, speaking in very good English, saying that the German submarines had sunk a number of American ships coming to Europe, and they would keep attacking us until every ship was sunk. She was boasting about the German successes to boost the morale of the German people.

When we arrived at Liverpool, I was ordered to Northern Ireland where we had our first troops stationed, and I served there until the troops emptied out for the invasion of North Africa. Then, I was ordered to England, where I was stationed at the American Army cemetery in Brookwood, near Surrey. They carried out funerals three days a week—on Tuesdays, Thursdays and Saturdays—but I told them there should be no Jewish burials on Saturdays. That gave me five days that I could travel throughout England and Scotland to visit bases and to meet with Jewish troops and officers and conduct services.

After the Normandy invasion in June of 1944, I became very busy at the Brookwood cemetery. With the first landings at Normandy, we were busy burying men, sometimes as many as 300 or 350 a day. I would make certain that I had a Catholic chaplain and a Protestant chaplain present, and bulldozers would dig long trenches. The bodies were carefully prepared, and carefully placed in the trench. And when all of the bodies were placed in the trenches, each of the three of us conducted his own religion's burial service. It was difficult emotionally, and that happened day after day. There was no burial place as of yet in France, so that continued for quite a while.

And then in August of '44, I was ordered to Normandy. . . . In the Army, you're supposed to help men of all faiths who come to you for counseling. The only distinction would be the service of a particular faith. I had Catholic and Protestant soldiers who came to me for counseling, if I happened to be the chaplain closest. . . . Soldiers were much more open to faith in times of danger than people are generally, and the attendance at services was always good. I have no doubt that having a deeper faith helped these soldiers go on. . . . We knew the business we were in—it wasn't child's play. We knew that a good number of the men were going to die. We hoped that we wouldn't be one of them—chaplains were being killed too.

The only time I was actually close to death during the war was in Normandy, when I was with my Catholic senior chaplain, and his deputy. . . . I was sitting in the front seat with the driver, and the two more senior officers were in the rear. We were going through the woods when we heard the crack of a rifle. And I suddenly felt a cold wind go past the back of my neck. And the two officers said, "Wow, that bullet just missed you!" . . .

In the summer of 1945, I was sent to Frankfurt, Germany, by orders of General Eisenhower. When I arrived, I was told that I had a new job. I was to travel to displaced persons camps—DP camps—to meet with Jewish survivors who had been liberated by the American army from the German concentration camps, in order to find out what the needs of these survivors were and to report that to General Eisenhower. . . .

I was horrified by what I saw. No one had told us that there were concentration camps. On one of my first trips, I went to Dachau, before it was cleaned up. I walked into a large room, and it had a lot of clothing hooks on the wall, and there was a nice polite German sign that said, "Remove your clothes, hang them on the hook, and remember where the hook is so that you can get your clothes afterwards, and then proceed to the showers." Then I went into the supposed shower room, and I see to my horror that it's what I had been told about. It was a gas chamber. I looked at the door through which I had just come—the heavy metal door—and I looked at the inside, and it was covered by scratches from top to bottom. I at once knew what they were. They were made by people. When the gas had been thrown in from the top, they were desperate in their futile attempt to get out, scratching at the door.

From there, I was sent into the next room, where there were three large furnaces, a crematorium. The bodies were carried from the gas chamber and shoveled into these furnaces. At the back of the room there were large sacks that looked like potato sacks. I looked to see what was in them, and I saw that they were still filled with what I'd seen in the bottom of the furnace: human ash. Each sack had been stamped in German on the outside, "Fertilizer." The ash was to be used to fertilize German farms. I rolled up my sleeve and plunged my arm into one of these sacks. I rubbed the ash against the palm of my hand with my fingers so that I should never forget what my eyes had seen there. As you can see, I have never forgotten. . . .

When I came back to the States, I did not know whether I could continue serving as a rabbi. In my own mind, I was wrestling with the idea that of course occurs to any person who believes in God—how could a good God permit this to happen? Fortunately, I was asked to be a fund-raiser, a speaker, by the United Jewish Appeal, which sent me on a six-month speaking tour in 40 states to speak at mass meetings of

American Jews to tell them what my eyes had seen and what I had done. When those six months were over, I was asked to go to South Africa to speak to the Jewish communities there for the same purpose. By that time, I had in my own mind resolved my difficulties. I simply said to myself, "If I believe in God I have difficulty. If I don't believe in God, I have more difficulties." . . .

I have no doubt that the war experience affected me as a rabbi. It made me see life whole, with its good and its evil. It made me see how wonderful human beings can be—how heroic, and how evil.

THE ONLY CONGRESSIONAL MEDAL OF Honor awarded to a chaplain went to Father Joseph O'Callahan, a professor at Holy Cross. His nephew, Jay O'Callahan, wrote this narrative about his uncle.

Just before World War II, two professors were arguing at Holy Cross College. One of them was Joseph T. O'Callahan, mathematics professor, and he was saying, "I don't know, I love teaching, but I've got to leave."

"What are you talking about, Joe?"

"I'm talking about the war. I'm talking about Hitler raging over Europe. We're just about to go to war. There are going to be a million kids involved. What am I doing safe in a classroom? If I were a chaplain, I could at least be some kind of help to those kids."

"Come on, Joe. You're thirty-six years old. You've got claustrophobia so bad you can barely stand under an umbrella. You've got high blood pressure and poor eyesight. You're a priest and a professor of mathematics. Let somebody else comfort the kids, Joe. Somebody who could lend a hand in an emergency."

Four years later, you, Lieutenant Commander O'Callahan, are on an aircraft carrier, the USS *Franklin*—Big Ben, they call her. It's seven in the morning March 19th, 1945, you're fifty miles off the coast of Japan. Every eye scans the sky nervously, afraid a Japanese plane is going to break through the air cover and drop a bomb. Just after seven in the morning, a Japanese plane does break through. It flies fifty feet above the deck of the *Franklin* and drops two 500-pound bombs.

One bomb drives through the flight deck. Then it drives through the fo'c'sle deck and finally explodes on the hangar deck. In moments, the hangar deck is one massive flame. Everyone in the hangar deck is dead. One- and two-thousand-pound bombs burned loose from the planes are rolling on the hangar deck, beginning to explode. Bombs and rockets are exploding at the rate of one a minute. Hundreds of thousands of gallons of aviation fuel are creating an inferno. There are hundreds dead already, hundreds more burned and wounded, and through the smoke somebody yells, "Padre! Padre! Flight deck forward."

You, the padre, Joe O'Callahan, make your way through the choking smoke to the forward flight deck. You turn around, and see behind you eight hundred feet of the flight deck, a mountain of fire. The black smoke churns away in a huge dark plume rising to the sky. You turn and see before you one hundred feet of the flight deck still clear of flame. Men are lying, groaning, all over that part of the deck. Even out in the air the stench of burned flesh is terrible. You run over, kneel down and take a sailor's hand.

"Padre, we're dead," he says.

The explosions are so loud it is difficult to hear, but you know what he means. The ship has lost power; it is dead in the water. . . . The *Franklin* is drifting toward Japan. There is fire, smoke, and confusion everywhere. Suddenly, you understand what's so important. Communication has broken down. There's terror everywhere. If a sailor looks for a petty officer for leadership, the petty officer is probably dead or in shock from burns. If a petty officer looks for an officer, the officer is probably trapped below decks or floundering in the water. There is no leadership because nobody recognizes anybody. Not in that smoke, not with faces smeared with it. You, the padre, realize everyone can recognize that white cross on your helmet. So you rush down to the fo'c'sle. There are forty or fifty sailors standing there. Not just in terror. They are in awe. The ship is blowing itself apart.

"Lads, lads! Want to save our happy home?"

They gather 'round you as if you are a magnet. You lead them up to the flight deck and turn those men into firefighting parties. . . .

Now, on the *Franklin*, that March 19th, at 9:52 in the morning, comes the biggest explosion of the whole day. The whole ship is rocked. It's like an angry cat that takes a rat in its jaws and shakes it. One more explosion like that, and the whole ship will go down.

You, the captain, Les Gehres, look down from the bridge, and you see two enclosed gun turrets. There are flames all around those gun turrets. If the shells in those turrets explode, the ship might go down. Down below you see the padre, Joe O'Callahan, with a fire hose, leading a group of sailors right through the flames. The padre gets right to the first gun turret and opens the door.

You, the padre, don't want to step into that gun turret. You have claustrophobia and your flesh crawls at the thought of it. It's dark in there, and you're going to be trapped, but you force your body in. The sailors follow you. You lift up a five-inch 38 shell and hand it to the sailor next to you, who passes it down the line, saying, "Padre, praise the Lord and dump the ammunition."

You, Captain Gehres, turn to your XO, Commander Joe Taylor, and say, "Get a tow on this ship!" It's impossible without power. Impossible. But you're drifting. You're only forty miles off the coast of Japan. An air battle is going on above you. The Japanese will sink you unless you're towed out of here. So you say, "Get a tow on this ship!"

So you, the XO, run down to the fo'c'sle and manage to get eighty men. The USS *Pittsburgh* comes astern and hands over a cable. The men have got to drag that cable along the fo'c'sle. There's a huge loop on its end, and that loop has to be put around a great hook on the deck, and then the ship can be towed. But eighty men cannot move the cable. That cable is six inches of steel. It's a quarter-mile long. It weighs thirty tons. You'd need a thousand men. Eighty men cannot move it. But they must.

Now imagine you are Frank Frasure, and you're on that cable. You're a steward's mate, second class, and you're a black man. All by yourself you start to sing slowly, "We're gonna take this line, and make a tow. Heave, ho. It's time to get on home." One by one, the other black sailors join in the song, "We're gonna take this line, and make a tow.

Heave ho. It's time to get on home. Heave, ho." Now the white sailors begin to sing. There are eighty sailors, young men and some older officers, all on the cable, singing that song of yours, "We're gonna take this line, and make a tow. Heave ho. It's time to get on home. Heave!" You're beginning to move that tow line. It's impossible, but you are beginning to move it.

Now you, Captain Gehres, look down on that flaming, slanting deck. The ship is at a thirteen-degree list. It might capsize. You see a five-hundred-pound bomb slithering along that slippery flaming deck toward a hole. If it goes through the hole, it will explode in the fo'c'sle where those men are moving the tow line. They will die, and the ship will continue to drift. You, Captain Gehres, see six sailors run through the smoke and stop the rolling bomb. They stand the bomb up on end and even from up there you can see the sailors shaking because the bomb is hot and about to explode. Two officers run over,

234 / TOM BROKAW

kneel down, and try to defuse the
bomb, but can't because they are too
nervous. Then you, the captain, watch
the padre, Joe O'Callahan, run over to
the bomb. He stands right beside it and
folds his arms. Everybody calms down.
And they defuse the bomb.

April 3rd, the battered USS *Franklin*
steams into Pearl Harbor. It's been out
just one month. . . . The *Franklin* is in
Pearl Harbor only a few days when
the Navy says, "Take the *Franklin* to the
Brooklyn Navy Ship Yard." And so the
battered *Franklin* steams east almost
11,000 miles. . . . On May 17th, 1945, in
the Brooklyn Navy Ship Yard, on the
flight deck of the *Franklin*, awards are
being presented. "Klimkiewiez, Mor-
gan, Frasure . . ."

You, the padre, are standing on the
flight deck having to blink a lot. The
sun must be awfully bright. You're just a
little disappointed for your mother, because she's just come aboard. And you
know your name is not going to be
called out today. You know your mother

is going to say, "Well, I bet Joe did something."

What you, Joe O'Callahan, don't know is that the moment your mother came aboard, Les Gehres, the captain, went over to her and said, "I'm not a religious man. But I watched your son that day and I thought if faith can do this for a man, there must be something to it. Your son is the bravest man I have ever seen."

On January 23, 1946, at the White House, President Harry S. Truman awarded Commander Joseph T. O'Callahan the Congressional Medal of Honor.

ANOTHER RECIPIENT OF THE CONGRESSIONAL Medal of Honor, Gino Merli, kept the faith after facing death again and again through a long night during the 1st Division's advance on Germany.

The night of September 4th, in Belgium somewhere, our company was ordered to stop the troops that were moving through Belgium and Germany—they were trying to get back to their homeland, the German soldiers were. And in the afternoon about six o'clock our company commander got notice saying that they needed a section of guns to set up a roadblock and 14 men to support it. They loaded up the two jeeps and we began marching towards the objective of the roadblock. We finally reach the town of Sars-la-Bruyère, and that's where [Sergeant] Patinski said, "This is where we set up the roadblock." So everybody got to work and then dug their foxholes, and we were prepared then to hold that roadblock at all costs. As we were digging our emplacement, the neighboring village citizens were coming over to the sergeant since he had the highest rank and telling him there were many, many enemy soldiers along that cobblestone road we came down. This is about 7:30 in the evening. Sergeant Patinski then sent a patrol out in front of the guns to see where the enemy was. They returned half an hour later and reported at least a hundred German soldiers marching down the road. Patinski got the two guns ready for an all-out stand to hold that roadblock.

When we opened fire in the first volley, the enemy soldiers coming down the cobblestone road were like ants. We couldn't believe our eyes when we saw the silhouette of the enemy soldiers—they were ahead [of] us, beside us, inside of us. We were holding the roadblock—by this time there were two of us that were killed, four injured, and many of the remaining had been taken prisoner. We were fighting under the cover of darkness. They came down four times to try to knock us off [the gun emplacement]. The last time they came around four A.M. and found the two lifeless bodies. We . . . my assistant gunner and myself . . . were stationed in our foxholes, the two of us. They turned around and left and said the job was done. No sooner had they turned around did we open fire—we killed them. . . . My assistant gunner was killed at this point. And so I stayed by myself.

Merli was now the only man on the machine gun in the foxhole. He pretended he was dead.

Another group came down later . . . they said something in German, I assume it was that nobody was there. So when they moved on, I opened fire by myself . . . from my foxhole. Later . . . I realized that there was this one German soldier left, out twenty yards in front of the gun emplacement. . . . He was wounded . . . but he knew that I was there. . . . I could hear him moving, calling to his comrades that he was wounded. He was moving and I was moving. We knew the other was there. . . . So from four a.m. to six a.m. he knew I was alive and I knew he was alive. He was watching because . . . there was a bright moonlight that night and you could see an outline of a human being. So he was watching for me . . . watching for my silhouette. . . . He tried to shoot once.

Then his medic came to help him, and he tried to convince his own medic that there was someone still alive at the position. But the medic didn't believe his own soldier, and said "We don't have time to worry about one man in a fox-hole." . . . I can vividly remember now every move, every second from eight that evening to nine the next morning. You had to stay alive, stay awake, if you wanted to survive. . . .

Finally, at dawn, Merli's outfit rescued him.

The morning after, they took us to the chow house and there was breakfast. And afterwards I asked Sergeant Patinski if he wouldn't mind if I went and prayed for the dead—our dead and their dead. No matter how bitter you were against the enemy, you still had the heart to pray for him. Because he was in the same boat as you and I . . . We went to the small church nearby and sat down and said some prayers. . . . The sergeant came with me, and one or two others of the squad came with me. We prayed in silence . . . I'd say for a good 15 minutes. I was thinking of my assistant gunner who was killed. . . .

I prayed for the ones that lost their lives that night. But I also prayed for that one wounded soldier who waited and waited to find my silhouette. But that never happened. And thank God it didn't. That's why I went to the church and prayed. I felt that if anybody out there was given a chance to knock me off that gun emplacement, it was that German soldier. . . . I still think about him. . . . Many, many times I've felt that this individual who lived through four o'clock to six o'clock—that he is looking for me, somewhere, somehow. . . . I've always felt that he is out there looking for me. . . .

RITA VALDRINI MORASCO OF PITTSBURGH
WAS part of a personal and spiritual pilgrim-
age with her husband, Robert, in search of
his father, who was killed in combat.

I thought you might be interested in a
no less than miraculous event which
brought together, after 50 years, a father
and son mortally separated by WW II
German gunfire. The event evolved
from a trip my husband and I made in
the mid-'90s to visit my extended family
in northern Italy.

50 years ago at that time, on February
4, 1945, my husband's father, Robert
Anthony Morasco, was gunned down
on La Serra mountain by enemy mortar
fire while trying to free the little town of
Pianosinatico and the surrounding
countryside from German occupation.
Robert was a Private, First Class, of the
elite infantry group, the 10th Mountain
Division of the United States Army.

We had hoped to "know" Robert better by immersing ourselves in history itself. And this would be made possible

for us with the assistance of my Italian cousin from Genoa, a Jesuit priest, who could serve as translator for us in our travels.

We arrived in Pianosinatico with my cousin the next day to be greeted by the community elder, who had prepared dinner in her home for us, and this special "someone" by the name of Valerio Petrucci, a quiet, sweet-looking 67-year-old man with a gentle voice. The following is his revelation to us:

Valerio was 17 when his home town of Pianosinatico was finally freed from occupation when the German forces in Italy surrendered to Allied forces on May 2, 1945. And it was late May of that year, as the snows in this mountain tower were finally melting, that Valerio made a life-changing discovery while picking mushrooms in the woods high above his parents' home.

In a small clearing, he found, separated by several hundred yards, the bodies of two individuals who he knew were American soldiers because of the color of their uniforms. The one body had apparently been exposed to the sun for some time because the body was partially decomposed. The soldier had been severely wounded in the head. His spectacles and a bullet-ridden helmet lay nearby.

Several hundred feet from the first soldier, Valerio found the body of the second. This soldier was lying about 10 feet from the edge of a cliff overlooking the town.

This second soldier was lying on his side with his head tilted back and facing upward toward the sky. His mouth was open, and Valerio recalled that the teeth he could see were straight and even. The soldier had been severely wounded in the side and the wound was packed with gauze bandages that were now stained with blood. The soldier had apparently received medical attention for a time following his wounding . . . until he died. This soldier also bore no identification.

But *we* knew his name.

Valerio said that, over the years, he has frequently returned to that clearing to light a cigarette and to ponder his sacred discoveries. He said that for 50 years he has imagined what it would be like to meet the families of those two brave, fallen American soldiers who sacrificed their lives for his people. He wept heavily as he gazed at my husband.

And we did return in September of the following year. We brought with us a bronze ground marker on which was inscribed in Italian, in addition to Robert's name and date of death, "Mortally wounded for the liberation of Pianosinatico." We would place the marker on the exact spot indicated by Valerio.

About 30 townsfolk met us at our hotel in the mountains and walked with us up the mountain. One old soldier had been completely blinded in the war, and his daughter and son-in-law assisted him in his ascent of the mount. We were profoundly touched by his presence. People brought beautiful fresh-cut flowers, the American and Italian flags were carried, and one man in his 60's made the trek with a wooden altar on his back for the celebration of mass at the top. The climb took an hour.

As we rounded the summit and stepped into a small clearing about 50 feet from the edge of the mountain, we looked into the blue heavens beyond, high above the town of Pianosinatico below. Piercing the infinity of that blue sky was a 7-foot wooden cross rising majestically from the precipice . . . a 7-foot cross erected in the previous months by Valerio, his nephew and some local artisans to mark the spot where Valerio had found Robert so many years ago. At the base of the cross was a stone monument with an Italian inscription, "As the sun rises, so it illuminates Your glory." I began to cry. My husband wept, too, as we stood there holding each other. It was deeply moving to think that Robert's body, alone for so long, alone as his wife was giving birth back home to his child, many a morning greeted the sun as it rose over that precipice. Yes, his body, alone, greeted the sun, but his spirit had long been with God.

We return every year to that town, to that mountain. We all make the journey, together with Valerio, his wife and son, the priest, soldiers, and many townspeople. Advance notice of our coming is announced in the local newspaper so that townspeople can plan their schedules to be with us. We meet at the base of the mountain, walk together upwards, celebrate mass at the foot of the cross, talk about the war and what town residents remember or have heard from others about that time in 1945, and afterward, for a day or two, visit with the many new friends we have made and "family" my husband has finally found for himself in Italy.

My husband still loves to hear his mom tell of her romance with Robert . . . how handsome and dashing he was, how intensely patriotic, idealistic and good. He was the stuff that an heroic tale is made of. But now he is even better than that. Now, 54 years after Robert lay dying on foreign soil, 54 years after the birth of the son of whom he only dreamed and who would bear his full name, 54 years after the end of that horrible war, U.S. Army Pfc. Robert Anthony Morasco, I do believe, is looking down with a father's love and pride on the son who cared to share with him the final moment of life.

We thank Robert for his sacrifice . . . and we salute him in love.

V

REUNIONS

Thomas J. Broderick, Joseph P. Wall, Linda Murphy, Margaret Ray Ringenberg, Dorothy Dowling, Peggy Assenzio, James Dowling, John Assenzio, Maureen Caulfield, John "Lefty" Caulfield—guests at the 1999 meeting of the USS Missouri Association

An American ritual—little known by those who do not participate—is the annual reunion of military units from World War II. Foot soldiers and sailors, pilots and tank drivers, rear-echelon outfits and battle-scarred companies are bound together by their common experience during W.W. Two, as they like to call it.

The reunions are getting smaller now. Some men prefer not to attend. The memories of war are too painful, or their new wives don't understand the appeal, or their postwar lives never measured up to that distinctive time when they were all together, doing something so dangerous, so adventurous, and so honorable.

Jack Van Ingen, a retired lieutenant colonel, wrote to tell me about the reunion of the 457th B-17 Bomb Group in Gettys-

burg, Pennsylvania; R. L. Rimmer was in the
Coast Guard, and his Patrol Frigate Association met in Atlanta in the summer of 1999;
the 194th Field Artillery Battalion met in
Amana, Iowa, on Labor Day weekend 1999
to talk over old times. The V-12 Sailors and
Marines of Colorado College, Colorado, an
officer training program, got together in the
fall of 1999. Joe Liberto invited me to a
Philadelphia reunion of the 607 Graves Registration Company, the men who had the
grim task of collecting the dead on D-Day
beaches and helping to establish the first
permanent American cemeteries in France.
The list goes on and on, through all the
branches of the service, from the celebrated
outfits to the obscure.

I wish that I could attend them all. Instead, I have chosen a few that are repre-
sentative of the personal reunions that grew
out of *The Greatest Generation*.

Lee Stratton Walter of Perkasie, Pennsylvania, wanted to tell us about her husband's
war buddy.

Trusting that you are not too overcome
with stories to hear another, here is one

that portrays how the human experience spills over again and again.

You can imagine that the wife of a WWII flier has heard fifty years full of war, and then some. So I was not at all surprised when someone called my husband, George, announcing that he was a WWII buddy. It was August of 1981. I was in the stable saddling up one of my horses, and my husband was up a hill, across the lawn, in the driveway. I went to the door and shouted, "There's someone named Ervie Cloyd on the phone. Says he was in the war with you." My husband returned dryly, "That's not possible. Ervie Cloyd is dead. Shot down over Romania!" Nevertheless, he had dropped everything and taken off, full throttle, for a house phone.

I would soon learn that Cloyd, one of my husband's tent mates in Italy, had come east from Arizona to attend a reunion of the Association of Former Prisoners of War of Romania, in Cherry Hill, New Jersey.

Although my husband had not been a POW, we were invited to attend. The guest of honor was Princess Catherine Caradja of the Romanian Royal Family, who at that time was in her eighties. She had assisted Allied fliers shot down in her country, insisting they were prisoners of Romania, to keep them from being captured and sent to Germany. She had also taken food to those imprisoned in Bucharest.

And the Princess went on to locate scores of former POW's, whom she referred to as "her boys."

Al Feliksa of Saint Ignace, Michigan, writes about his reunion with an RAF pilot whom he helped rescue from the Adriatic Sea in 1945.

Rather than destroying lives in battle, I had the privilege of being part of the 1st Emergency Rescue Squadron, whose task was that of rescuing air crews that were shot down and ejecting over water.

During WWII, our Search and Rescue crew was assigned to the US Army

12th Air Corps, based on a 15th Army Air Corps Field at Falconara, Italy. Our orders came from the British Command. We flew in Navy PBY-5A's (Army number OA-10A). On March 14, 1945, we were patrolling over the northern part of the Adriatic Sea. A radio message informed us that a fighter pilot was shot down off the coast of Venice and gave us the pilot's approximate location. Our on-board radar pinpointed the pilot in the water and the rescue was successful in spite of heavy shore battery cannon fire causing some damage to our aircraft.

He was a Jewish pilot in the South African Air Force and flew with the British Royal Air Force out of Italy. While flying a British Spitfire and strafing and bombing anti-aircraft installations at Madre, a city near Venice, his plane was hit by anti-aircraft fire, but he managed to climb to 5,000 feet before bailing out into the icy cold Adriatic. I often wondered what happened to the downed pilot. I never knew his name . . . but somehow he remembered mine.

THEN—after 53 years, came a voice out of the past. It was a letter from that rescued pilot, Boris Senior. . . . He located me through Jim Thompson and Jim Morrison, founders of the PBY Catalina International Association, of which I am a member.

Boris Senior described his life after his rescue.

After World War II, I went to England to study at London University, but after learning about the murder of six million Jews in the Holocaust (about one third of the entire Jewish population of the world), I felt unable to continue to study and went immediately to Palestine to prepare for the War of Independence in 1948, hoping to ensure the creation of a safe homeland for Jews from anywhere. Together with a small number of volunteers we started the Israel Air Force, flying what was available, at first even dropping bombs we carried in our laps.

In time, we managed to get fighter aircraft, strangely enough Messerschmidt 109's made in Czechoslovakia, which I flew against the Egyptian Spitfires. I went through the entire war plus more years in 1956, 1967, and 1973.

Feliksa concludes:

Boris recently retired as a leader of the present Israeli Air Force. By the sound of his life, he led a significant role in establishing and keeping Israel a solid nation. I told him that I thanked GOD that he survived the war and had an opportunity to live a full and meaningful life.

WHEN HE ATTENDS THE REUNION OF HIS World War II outfit, Marty Fritz of Northfield, Massachusetts, who has been a farmer for fifty years, can look back on a long life of poverty, hard work, and pride.

I was born May 22nd, 1922, the oldest of 6 children. My dad was working 6 days a week for $17.00. Memories of the depression years are still so vivid in my mind. We lived close to the railroad tracks in the poor section of town. I went to Catholic school taught by the Sisters of Saint Joseph [and that time] has long since blessed me with many fond memories of my formative years.

When I came home from school my mother would make me change my clothes right through to the skin and put on old clothes. We had to save our good clothes for church and school. After which I would take pails and walk the railroad tracks, picking up coal that fell off all the coal cars heading North. I would pick coal until dark. When I came home with the coal, I would find my younger brothers whining, "Mama, I'm hungry." I would ask my mother, "Ma, what's for supper?" She would snap back, "Wind pudding and air sauce." I would then find her crying. I felt so bad.

When I was a freshman in high school, I became acquainted with a farmer who needed help on his farm. He told me he would pay me $15 a month. I talked my folks into letting me go there, thinking my share could go to my brothers and sisters. I had to get up at 4:00 A.M., work in the barn until 6:30, run up the house, change my clothes, have my breakfast, then walk two miles to meet the school bus. After school, the same walk back. I had to work in the barn until 9:00 P.M. Then to the woodshed to split.

On Sundays I walked 7 miles to go to church. When I got paid, I gave my mother $10. With the $5.00 I had left I bought and paid for my own clothes. I worked on that farm for five years. The last 6 months I worked for the farmer, he had no money to pay me. On the night of December 7, 1941, lying on my bed listening to music on the radio, the music stopped. They said, "We interrupt this program to bring you a special news bulletin. The Japanese have bombed Pearl

Harbor." I did not even know where Pearl Harbor was. All night I listened to all the reports coming in from all across the Pacific. In view of the fact that I had not been paid in 6 months, and [the farmer] owed me $90, I thought it was time for me to change course. The next day I asked the man I was working for if he would mind if I had the day off. I walked 7 miles to enlist in the U.S. Navy. After 6 weeks at the Naval Training Station in Newport, R.I., I was assigned to the new battleship U.S.S. *Massachusetts,* where I served 4 years.

I will be forever so grateful that I had the honor and the privilege to serve my beloved country in her hour of need. To this very day I still thank God for helping us win the war, and for the great leaders we had at that time. The admiral, the generals, and all the fine young men, and women, who laid their lives on the line to preserve our precious freedom.

After I returned home from the war I met, and later married, a wonderful lady "like your mother." I was indeed truly so blessed. We were married 50 years last April 24. We have three lovely daughters and two grandchildren. I have been farming for 50 years. With God's help, I am still farming.

I went to my ship's 53rd reunion last June. So many of my wonderful friends and old shipmates now dwell in the house of the Lord forever. As each one takes leave they seem to take a piece of me with them.

ONE REUNION THAT DIDN'T HAPPEN SADDENS me. It would have involved my late father-in-law, Merritt Auld, a battalion surgeon who died in 1980. Molly Hunter and Krista Markway, the granddaughters of Marcellus Markway of Jefferson City, Missouri, wrote to tell me of Markway's assignment as an ambulance driver for Dr. Auld.

When we were in high school, we were required to interview a World War II veteran for our American History course. Of course, we interviewed our grandpa and it was always a difficult and emotional time for him. He just would not open up about his experiences. So we learned that the war was not a subject to approach Grandpa about. Then your book was published. He received the book as a gift and began reading it (though many of us doubted that he would). Since the day that he began reading it, our grandpa has changed. The book is now dog-eared, placed prominently on the table next to his reclining chair. There are all sorts of markers hanging out of it, including the list of the men that he served with. He even marks up the pages, underlining names and places.

Now when we go to visit him, he talks to us about his experiences. He once told us that his commanding officer or company leader (we are not sure of the title), Dr. Merritt Auld, is one of the finest men he has ever known. That in itself is a tremendous compliment coming from our grandfather, who is a loving

Christian and father, a good judge of character and the most talented worker that we have ever seen. Grandpa now tells us stories about the war, shares a scrapbook filled with pictures and all sorts of mementos that have been hidden for years, and has a look of pride in his eyes that we have never seen.

Mary Beth Markway Rieke, the daughter of Mr. Markway, wanted to share a war story involving her father, which later led to a reunion.

One day he was driving his ambulance on the beautiful hillsides of rural Italy. Bombers and machine gunners appeared overhead. He ran for cover in the only place he could find—a church, under the altar stone. Waited there several hours until the bombing and machine-gunning subsided. Felt it safe to radio his captain, Merritt Auld. (He has a small photo of the church and his ambulance, both pierced with hundreds of bullet holes.)

[To Auld he said:] "Sir, I'm stranded. All tires on my ambulance shot out. Need four new tires."

A couple hours later a shining faced private, Freddy St. John, showed up with four new tires.

Recently Mother told me this story: A month ago she was at home in the house that my dad had built for them. There was a knock at the door. An older fellow, it was Mr. Fred St. John, from Georgia. He was looking for my dad, Mark.

I'm sorry, my mom says, he's not here now, he's playing cards with his friends at the bowling alley.

Mr. St. John asks directions and goes to the bowling alley. Walks in. Sees my dad. Says, "Who are you?" to my dad.

My dad, not quite recognizing him, doesn't give his real name, lightly jokes.

Mr. Fred St. John says, "You're Mark."

"What's your name?" says my dad.

"I'm Freddy St. John."

They hadn't seen each other since that day so long ago. Mr. St. John had come to see my dad because as young men 56 years ago they had met when my dad needed four new tires on the war-torn hillside of rural Italy, and a deep, deep bond of human gratitude and glory was formed.

Mary Kay Duckworth, Markway's sister, picked up the narrative in her letter about the 109th Medical Battalion of the 34th Infantry Division.

What really impressed me was his close friendship with his fellow soldiers in a medical company, made up mostly of National Guard members from Iowa. The group of farm boys soon made and have retained lifetime connections. Throughout the war years his letters were a running commentary on the incidental daily happenings, often mentioning by name his good friends. Thus, they became our acquaintances also.

Having experienced the war together, it is a blessing for these men to retain a warm and close relationship today. I ex-

perienced this on a trip through Iowa in
the fall of 1998 with him and his wife.
We had wonderful meals and good visits with his wartime friends in their
homes, and at the local cafés. These ap-
pointments were set up the night before by telephone as we traveled the
highways and byways of Iowa. Usually
the men gathered together and perhaps
reminisced while the ladies got reacquainted . . . these visits had continued
over the years. We "toured" homesites,
witnessed their various hobbies and in-
terests, shared family news, important
and not-so important news . . . good
conversations. I have never met more
quality-minded, personable individuals,
now in their eighties.

VI

---•---

LOVE
STORIES

The last family photograph of Helen, Sandra, and John Chichilla, 1944.

George A. Yates, U.S. Navy, with his bride-to-be, Juanita Greenwell.

Mr. and Mrs. Joe DeMaggio, November 11, 1945.

In researching *The Greatest Generation,* I quickly discovered that almost every war story had a love story connected with it. That led to a chapter called "Love, Marriage, and Commitment."

The chapter, in turn, elicited more love stories from the men and women of that generation. It does seem that the common struggles, the risks, the long separations at an early age, the relief of survival did forge some uncommonly strong marriages. Those couples look back on their lives together and count the durability of their union and the family it produced as their greatest achievement.

To be sure, there were failures. Passions born of youth, war, and the prospect of early death led to whirlwind romances and quickie marriages before a man was shipped overseas. But once the war was over, it was sometimes difficult to reignite those fires. Some men returned from war hardened, troubled, abusive, unable to stay in a loving relationship or fit in to a life with softer edges. Marriage counseling and other forms of psychological help were not widely available in the immediate postwar years.

So it is all the more a wonder that many marriages did endure, did flourish, especially when so many of them were embarked upon when the couples were of tender age, with little or no experience in the grown-up world they were expected to inhabit.

After a long lifetime together their love affair has come full circle. As they were once giddy with anticipation about their common future, now they have the quiet satisfaction of a promise kept.

JUANITA YATES OF MONROE CITY, MISSOURI, lived happily with her husband's other love: his time in the U.S. Navy.

My husband, George A. Yates, Petty Officer First Class (cook), was in the

Navy four and one-half years and spent three and one-half years on the destroyer USS *Badger* 126, most of it in the North Atlantic protecting supply ships headed for the Allied troops. He died September 18, 1997. I lived with the love of his life, the U.S. Navy, as my only competitor for his affections for 52 years. The 11 children, 36 grandchildren, and four great-grandchildren were raised to "swab the deck, fore and aft, bulkhead to bulkhead," and we always ate in the galley rather than the kitchen. Sound familiar? They knew his stories by heart and he was always ready for another telling.

George died of congestive heart failure and was on a heart pump, but we were privileged to care for him at home the last six months of his life. A farmer and salesman of farm machinery, he literally worked the day he died, from his bed. A man called that morning with something wrong with his machine and George told him how to fix it over the phone. So weak he could hardly talk, he handed the phone to me and said, "I knew I could still do it." A few hours later he was dead.

What a privilege we had. Constantly surrounded by family, he would tell his Navy stories to yet the third generation on any occasion. At 4 A.M. the family was still there when he breathed his last. We got to say our goodbyes, listen to his advice whether we wanted to or not, and hear him say how much he loved all of us. It was easier then than in his early years when he worked so hard and the emotion was buried so deep. He was a deeply religious man, grateful to his God that his life had been spared. Those last eight hours were full of prayer, tears and a lot of laughter. Oh, how he loved to laugh!

You, George, and they truly were the greatest generation.

SOME WIVES STILL MARVEL AT THE ABILITY OF their combat veteran husbands to see everything in life after the war as a dividend. One of those wives is Dorothy A. Talbott of Golden, Colorado.

My husband and I have both read your book, and found it very interesting and heart warming. It did take us back a few years!

My husband, John, is almost 76 years old, was a "Depression kid" who went to New Mexico Military Institute in the thirties (courtesy of a great-uncle), then to OCS, and on to the Tenth Mountain Division at Camp Hale, Colorado. He got there because he had worked with horses at NMMI, so was sent to Camp Hale as a "mule officer" only to discover that they'd done away with mules some time before! So, they put him in a line company, because he'd written on his info sheet that one of his hobbies was skiing, even though he'd only been once! He was transferred out (before the Tenth went overseas) as a replacement officer in the Massachusetts National Guard, and eventually to the Battle of the Bulge in Europe. He was wounded (his helmet saved his life from a hand grenade), and after recovering in England was with the occupation forces, and spent some time in

Munich as a censor for a German newspaper (he'd learned German at NMMI).

I am 70 years old, was also a "Depression kid," whose banker father had lost everything in the crash. I, however, was in high school during the war, and graduated in 1946, and am appalled now at how unaware I was while the war was going on. We didn't have TV then, of course, and I suppose I was a typical teenager—not terribly interested in much beyond my own small world. . . .

The real purpose of this letter is to tell you that until I read your book (reinforced the other night by your interview), I never really understood the impact that the war must have had on my husband. I'm sure that his experiences in military school and the army molded his character like nothing else. And it explains why he has conducted himself with such courage battling a neuromuscular disease for the last forty-two years. He was diagnosed with a form of muscular dystrophy, called spinal muscular atrophy, when he was 34. It was very slow progressing, and he even skied until he was in his fifties. However, he's been quite disabled for the last ten years or so, and can do very little for himself. He was a stockbroker when diagnosed—thank goodness—because he didn't have to change occupations. He's just made his living on the telephone all these years, and is STILL working (although finally has decided to retire the end of the year). He's truly an inspiration to all who know him, because he's always cheerful, never complains, and only occasionally gets angry at something he can't do (but only I overhear that!). So, this has been truly the biggest battle of his life, and he has managed it remarkably well, with great dignity and grace. I think that his war experiences really pale in comparison, because this has gone on so long.

JOE DEMAGGIO OF ALBUQUERQUE, NEW Mexico, described how he and his wife,

Anne, were married and included a poem one of their children wrote for their fiftieth wedding anniversary.

On December 7, 1941, my girl friend and I had gone to the movies for her birthday and [were] faced with the truth when the picture was stopped, the lights went on and the theatre manager announced that all military personnel had been ordered to their commands immediately. When we came out of the theatre the newspaper boys were telling the story of the Japanese attack on Pearl Harbor. We had been dating for about a year and a half and looking forward to a married life together. However, I was expecting to be drafted and decided that I would not put my wife at the risk of becoming a widow. We [remained] engaged and two months later, February 6, 1942, I reported to the Induction Center and [was] sent to Camp Upton, Long Island, N.Y., and then on to Fort McClellan, Alabama, for basic infantry training. . . .

When the war ended in Europe, our battalion was in the vicinity of Kassel awaiting the possibility of going home after thirty-nine months of overseas duty. Instead, our Battalion Commander informed us that our next move would be to the Pacific. I immediately wrote to my fiancee and told her not to wait for my return because I didn't expect to survive such a mission. Thanks to the A bomb our battalion was ordered to the coast of France for demobilization. I was discharged on October 11th and Anne and I were married on November 11th, Armistice Day.

We have been married for 53 years and have been blessed with two children and three grandchildren of whom we are very proud. On our 50th Anniversary, which was attended by about 75 people, including family and friends from many parts of the country, we were presented with the enclosed "Now We Are One," written by our son, Paul, and I was asked to read it aloud for everyone to hear. I was doing fine

until the last paragraph when the lump
in my throat was choking me.

*Their Parents Came from Foreign
   Lands,*
In Search of "the Dream."
They were to work at the early age,
*But also to learn and be the best they
   could.*
*Their Papas and Mamas taught them to
   be as One.*

They Played With Cans, Sticks, Rocks,
*whatever imagination could fabricate for
   fun.*
*They met at work and enjoyed friend-
   ship, while*
*earning their way as their parents had
   done.*

*The War Disrupted Their Fun With
   Duty,*
Honor and Love of Country.
*One of them would fight the war on
   foreign soil,*
put his life on the line for a future.
*One would work in the factories at
   home*
and pray for him to return there.

*They Were Apart, But Now They Were
  One.*

*Fifty Years of Their Life Together
with all of its meaning,
Bring us here to celebrate how Two
  became One.*

*Learn Life's Lesson, Never Forget,
How You Came to This Time & Place;
You Are Who You Are,
Because They Are One.*

WORLD WAR II MAY HAVE BEEN THE LAST
great age of the love letter. Love letters have
been written since, but never on such a
scale. Mail call for those in uniform and the
daily postal delivery for those at home were
cherished rituals of life. Those letters
brought news of family, neighborhood gos-
sip, confessions of loneliness and fear, expressions of sympathy from commanding
officers for families whose young men were
wounded or dead—the full spectrum of
human emotion, but most of all, love.

Patricia Matthews Dorph of Staten Island, New York, shared letters exchanged by
her parents during the war:

Both my parents grew up on Staten Island, just a few doors from one another. They attended the same grammar and high schools. When my father started Columbia University in 1935, my mother got a job in Manhattan. Not until senior year in Columbia did my father start his courtship with my mother. In 1939 my father started Columbia Law School. Probably one of the most magical days was August 23, 1941, when they were married. They lived near Columbia for almost a year until my father graduated from law school. Then the draft took him away to boot camp in July 1942. Officers Training School followed, where they lived together in Georgia for a few months. My father was sent overseas in July 1943—first to Iceland, then England, then, about a month after D-Day, he went to France. Some time was spent in Belgium and Germany. He was an officer assigned to Eisenhower's Communications Division.

My parents wrote almost every day. They not only wrote what was happening in their personal lives but their hopes, dreams, fears and most profoundly their love and dedication to one another. . . .

My father died at a young age in 1962. My mother raised the three of us always looking on the best side of life and instilling in us honesty, compassion and to live life to the fullest. No one could ever understand why my mother never dated or remarried. She had a lot to offer someone. It was not until I read all the hundreds of letters that they wrote to each other during the war that I realized that my father was my mother's one true love. No one could ever take his place.

Roger Matthews's nickname for his wife Sophie was Joe. This is a letter he wrote in August 1944.

Dear Joe,

I have shown your very fancy salutation to the proper people and they are impressed; must be convinced that you love me more than their gals love them. And incidentally, I know that they know that much as they might like some female, they can't even get near the way I feel about you. They should, anyway, because I mention it often enough. I suppose that my attitude may become boring to them at times but I have to tell someone about it, don't I? I have just heard a very familiar cry . . . a chorus by my friends who have just walked into the office . . . it is "Deeeearrrrrr Sophie!" That happens every time they see me at the typewriter. . . .

So you want to know what nights I go riding in the jeep? If I could count on meeting you, I would make it any night or any day. I would even *walk!* One year's being alone, when it hits you all at once, hurts a little, doesn't it. Aww, why feel sad; I'm going down and take a look at your picture. As long as I have you, nothing can be really wrong.

All my love,
Roger

At home, Sophie was volunteering to wrap bandages for the Red Cross, a vital chore that went on everywhere in America. Here is a letter she wrote Roger in August 1944.

My darling Roger. I'm very tired. It's 11:30 but I could not go to sleep without telling you how many dressings we made tonight. We broke all records. 3094 dressings for 21 workers in 3 hours—that's impossible but we did it. I'm a slave driver—you know me. . . .

Roger dear, the R.C. ladies all approve of your pictures. I'm getting such pleasure out of them dear. You sure minded all my instructions. I could just see you saying "Sophie wants me to smile and look pleasant"—You are an angel to do me such a favor. Good night my darling one. I love you so very much dear. Kiss me—your own dear,

Sophie

Here is a letter from Roger to Sophie, dated early August 1944.

Dear Sophie,

This is one letter you probably won't get for a long time—so now that you finally have it, I hope it lives up to your expectations.

At the moment I'm relaxing on a bunk with two more bunks over my head. Urg is in one, Willie in the other. Altogether there are 9 1st Lts. in this one stateroom. But we are getting along pretty well.

Maybe you've already guessed where I am. Correct—on a boat. Name, capacity, location, etc. all military secrets. I think I can say it's not moving.

But censorship doesn't affect my saying that I love you, does it? That's no military secret; in fact it's no secret at all. I keep loving you more and more, and now I'm really beginning to miss you.

Sophie to Roger, August 3, 1944:

My darling Roger—Today my joy at receiving two letters from you—my first since last Sat.—was rather dimmed by a very sad letter from Karolyn. Roger dear, Bill is missing in action since June 23rd. It was such a shock to me. He only went into action on June 17th. She said that there was a possibility of his being a prisoner because where he and his men were there was no identification of any kind at all found. I'm so sorry for her. She said though that Patsy was such a blessing now. I can well imagine. Needless to say, I wept some very wet tears. Maybe I'll get another letter soon giving me more information. Well dear, the pictures of you are enough to make even me happy. Such a lovely nice smile—the sun gleaming in your eyes. What do you mean by saying that you are funny looking. You are the handsomest feller in this whole army snooks.

Hey snooks—what are you practicing shooting for. Don't you know that I don't like such goings on? Guns are too dangerous and I don't want you to get too familiar with them. My angel, I think that you have gained some weight—

don't you? You look swell to me and I wish I could just hug you to pieces.

Roger to Sophie, August 13, 1944:

I have some letters of yours but the most important item in today's delivery was the anniversary card. A very nice looking one, of course, but the big thing was that it came. I will feel ashamed when you get the one I am sending to you; we can't get very fancy ones over here but I know that you will understand. It *is* the idea that counts, isn't it? I also have yours of the 2nd and 3rd of July. That was terrible news about Bill Quinlan and Karolyn must feel just [awful] about the loss, not knowing what to do. That's the worst thing about it; there is nothing that she can do but wait and hope that some good news will come out of it. I hope that's what happens. . . .

The worst part of war and being in it is not what may happen to you individually but what the effect will be on those that mean something to you. I realize more than ever now how much I love you and how much I want you to be happy. . . .

Art is now putting the pressure on me to get done with this and hand over the typewriter to him so that he can get to work on a letter to his wife. I told him that he has to wait so now he has gone outside and stolen another machine from somewhere. See how tenacious I am when I'm writing to you? Must be love.

> Love
> Kisses
> All kinds of stuff
> Roger

Roger to Sophie, August 26, 1944:

Dear Sophie,

OK! Don't go hitting me on the head! This will have to represent the letters for the 24th and 25th too. First of all, I am not where I used to be but I'm still not sure where I'm going. But since I won't be able to mail this anyway until we land, it's OK to say that it will be someplace in France. Now don't you start chewing on your nails! Of course, I don't actually know anything.

I've seen my first proof of how well the Allies have this sector of the world under control. It's amazing to see the number of ships, plying back and forth, just like a busy highway back home. It looks as though England ought to be emptied soon if it keeps up.

Remember what I said earlier—no worrying. I honestly can say that. And I love you very much and miss you even more.

All my love,
Roger

Roger to Sophie, August 31, 1944:

Dear Sophie,

As you can see we have finally got our various cases open and the typewriters are available again. Art is here with me busy on a letter to his wife, with a

French phrase book open before him. He wants to make her think that he is picking up the language rapidly. . . . That's the one out of which the *Stars and Stripes* picked the phrase "My wife doesn't understand me," for use of soldiers going to France, and got itself in a lot of trouble with many soldiers' wives! (You don't have to worry about that with me. The gals are around here are even less interesting than those who were in England.)

Good night, Joe
All my love,
Roger

Sophie to Roger, September 19, 1944:

Do you miss me today? I sure miss you. I've had an "experience" today. I think that I really hit bottom this morning. My nerves were all shot to pieces and I was shaking like a leaf. When Gussie called to say that there was a letter from you I was completely cured. What do you think it is snooks—love? I am getting pretty certain of the fact that I love you so much. Of course the news about Kent's death last night upset me quite a bit. I still don't realize it—even though I can say it.

Roger to Sophie, September 22, 1944:

Dear Sophie,

The letters are still arriving all out of order. The latest batch that I have to report are those of the following dates: August 26th, 29th, 30th, and 31st. And for all of them my sincerest thank-yous. Letters from you are the nicest things that I can get in France or England or any place else that you might think of. Just as soon as I get all of them gathered together from out of my various shirt pockets and field jackets I am going to line them up in order and read them all over again just to get a clear picture of what you really were doing the last few weeks of August. . . .

I had about ten minutes' worth of business out around Versailles today so

Rose and I went out, took care of the business and then took in the Chateau or whatever it should be called. Gosh, Hon, how I wish you could be here to get to places like that with me!

Sophie to Roger, June 19, 1945:

Roger dear—

How's my favorite friend this fine day! I've thought it all over very carefully and just decided that I like you more than anyone else in the whole wide world and want you home soon. Gets lonesome without you! . . .

Today is the day that NYC is welcoming Eisenhower. If it had been a regular parade I'd have gone but it was only a motorcade—zip, and it's over. Give me the old fashioned kind of a parade where the bigshot sits on the steps of St. Patrick's and watches the show go by.

Georgie's Purple Heart medal reached home today. A pretty fancy looking hunk of stuff. He'll be a fancy looking fancy when he gets home don't you think. I'll bet 5 cents he did not find you. Made a sort of a rush trip through Europe—don't you think?

On Friday, darling, it will be 3 years that you are in [the] U.S. Army. That was your induction date—remember? Also 3 years out of Law School—3 years on the 29th that you were admitted to the Bar—such a world. Gussie and Jack are married 4 years on Thursday. Does it seem real to you that we will be married 4 years by the end of summer? . . .

Our little Susan is rapidly becoming a Big Susan. We are going to weigh her again tonight. She's a doll and I love her. At first they sleep about 23 hours of the day but now she's awake for a few hours at a time and just lies still—no weeping—no nothing—just kicking and eating. . . .

I'll say, so long for a while my pet. You are my most favorite darling pet and I wish you were here because I'd like very much to neck with you.

Your own dear
Joe

Roger to Sophie, June 26, 1945:

SUBJECT: Report of Mission to PARIS, FRANCE

TO: COMMANDING OFFICER, 24 Dudley Ave. Detachment, Matthews Family, APO 1, Sunnyside, S.I.

THROUGH: The same old channels.

In that letter, Roger described in great detail his trip into Paris and included a hand-drawn map (opposite).

Roger and Sophie—Joe—did find their way back into each other's arms after the war and, as their daughter says, their romance continued.

NOT ALL OF THE LOVE LETTERS HOME HAD A happy ending. Sandra Eve MacDuffee's father, John Chichilla, was killed in 1945. His letters from the Christmas season of 1944 have a special poignancy.

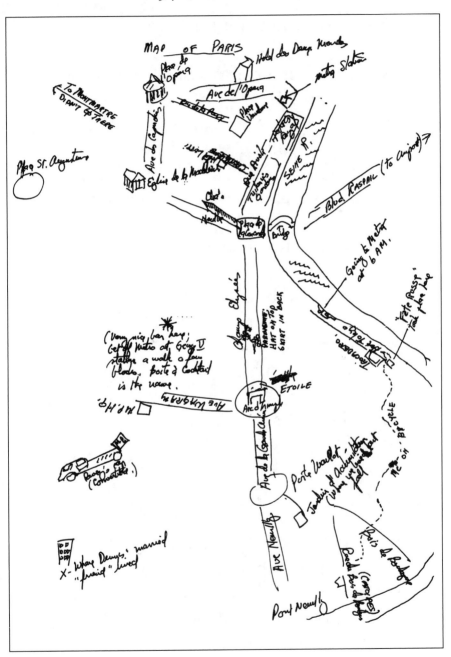

My dad was killed two days before my second birthday in 1945, so I have no memories of him, which to me is the saddest part of it all. I have a lot of pictures, thanks to my mom's diligence and she and I talked about him a lot as I got older. My dad is buried in a military cemetery in Luxembourg and when I was sixteen, my mom ordered an aerial photo of the cemetery with his cross circled in pencil. We also got a close-up snapshot of his cross that enables us to read his name and outfit. The day that picture arrived was a day of many tears for both Mom and me, and of an overwhelming sense of loss. . . .

I miss him more and more as I get older, not ever having known him and wondering what my life would be like today if he had come home safe.

My mom remarried, but she never stopped loving my dad and she never stopped grieving for him. Mom also had a "Lost Love Remembered" scrapbook full of newspaper clippings, cards from dad and photos of the two of them and me.

Nov. 15, 1944

Hello Darling,

Here I am sitting in a cellar safe as can be writing under a candle light. I love you, I adore you, my sweet Darling. Darling, Joe & I got split up yesterday, and to-day the fellow from New York & I got split up. So now I have two new pals—one from Idaho & one from Ohio, they are a lot of fun. . . . I love you darling wife, I adore you my sweet. A million hugs & kisses may God bless you & Sandra, I sure do miss you both my two sweet Darlings.

I love you, I love you, your loving husband,

Johnny

Nov. 27, 1944

Hello my little Sandra,

Sandra, how are you & Mother? Are you both well & pretty as you both were when I was home? I hope you are, because when I come home I am going to kiss the daylights out of you both. So,

Sandra, be a good girl to Mother & hurry up & learn to help Mother with the housework. I have a little toy dog I am going to send to you for a Christmas present. If I was home I would get a live dog for you. So you will have to wait until I come home. Sandra, give Mother a big kiss for me—also tell her that Daddy loves her with all of [his] heart. So long, my little daughter. Keep Mother happy for me. A million hugs & kisses to you and Mother & may God bless you both.

Your
Daddy

Dec. 28, 1944

Hello Darling,

. . . My Sweet Darling, I trust that you had a wonderful Christmas without me. As for me we spent Christmas eve & Christmas day in a fox hole. There [were] a lot of pine trees covered with snow surrounding us. At one thirty Christmas eve I was thinking of the last

Christmas when I went to the Midnight services & came home & found you listening to the radio. You had the services from St. Patrick's Cathedral in New York. I sat down & we both listened to it. After the service was over we listened to Bing Crosby sing Christmas carols. Christmas day I got out of my fox hole & sang a carol & went from one hole to another & wished the boys a Merry Christmas. So today we are going to have our Christmas dinner. . . .

My Sweet Darling wife, please don't worry about me because I am well & safe. But I need a shave & I am very dirty. So today I am going to clean up & it will be a relief to be clean again for a while. . . .

Darling, I love you so. All I ever dream & think of is the day that I come home & live peaceful again. So until then a million hugs, & kisses to you & Sandra. May God bless you both.

Your loving husband
Johnny

VII

APPRECIATION

Martha Barnett, president of the American Bar Association, 2000–2001, and Chesterfield Smith, president of the American Bar Association, 1973–1979

Terry Supple and the Gaynor Army

When I shared some of these stories with a friend, he was moved and then, after a moment, he commented on the nature of the world in which we live: "You hear something like that and you resolve to keep it in your mind forever, but twenty minutes later you're wondering what's for lunch." It was a thoughtful and perceptive comment on the pace of modern life and the selfish agendas that preoccupy too many of us.

Nonetheless, the stories in *The Greatest Generation* did strike a chord with many readers. Their response was uncomplicated and heartfelt. Both members of that generation and those who came later seemed grateful for the opportunity to say thank you, without apology or condition. Those expressions of appreciation came in a variety of forms and across generational lines.

Harold W. Duket of Nashotah, Wisconsin, wrote about how he felt after being thanked by a Vietnam veteran at a recent Memorial Day parade.

I am 76 years old, a veteran of the European Theatre of Operations and went in to Omaha Beach on the 14th of July, 1944 when the Germans were just six miles inland.

This past week ago Monday my wife and I attended the Memorial Day services at a small town in Wisconsin. As was my custom I wore my Eisenhower jacket (which I can get on but can't button) with my T5 rating on the sleeve along with 4 gold stripes for two years overseas and the few ribbons I picked up along the way and my overseas cap. I stood at the right times and saluted at the right times. As we got up to leave an army officer from the Vietnam conflict who had been on the band shell as one of the speakers came up to me and said: "I saw you in your uniform and I just wanted to say thank you."

It was later on that day when I realized he hadn't said "Thank you for coming to the ceremonies" or "Thank you for being here." He just said, "Thank you."

As I approach the 55th anniversary of my going ashore in France, I must say that this is the first time anyone ever said thank you for what we assumed was just our duty and obligation.

Douglas Barker of Groton, Massachusetts, wrote about his admiration for his father, William Barker, an Army lieutenant decorated for his service in Italy:

My father had a hankering to become part of the United States Army at a young age. He quickly enlisted the help of his parents in enrolling him at Valley Forge Military Academy. He graduated from the academy as a 2nd Lieutenant in the U.S. Army Infantry and left for North Africa and Italy in 1944.

My father had a knack for leading as well as staying alive. Throughout his campaigns he led his "E" Company valiantly through battles in North Africa and up into Italy. He was lucky in the respect that he had a company full of good men and a guardian above looking after him and most of his troops. . . .

During this Italian campaign he was awarded the Distinguished Service Cross for extraordinary heroism in action at the first battle of Cassino. He was later awarded the Bronze Star, the Purple Heart (with four clusters) and two invasion arrowheads. He was also awarded the Military Cross of Valour and the Bronze Medal for Valour by the Italian government.

The fifth time my father was wounded was somewhat of an end to his active military career. A barrage of incoming artillery shells turned out to be friendly fire that had missed its mark. While [he was] surveying the combat scene a shell dropped in front of him within ten yards' distance. He instinctively covered his face behind his arm as he heard the shell come in and explode. A large shell fragment ripped through his forearm and ricocheted off his helmet. Fortunately, after years and rounds of surgery he was able to recover 80% usage of his arm. . . .

I have enclosed, as well, a picture of my father as he returned from his tour of duty back in 1945. His left arm is in a cast from his shoulder to his wrist, his right leg in a steel brace due to bone and skin grafts. . . .

I am still to this day amazed and honored that the man in this picture (Captain William R. Barker, "E" Company, 2nd Battalion, 141st Infantry, 36th Texas Infantry Division), at 19 years of age, volunteered and went to war, fought for our country and returned home to build a successful business career; all in what amounted to be little more than just a fraction of his lifetime. Truly great accomplishments in my book.

An unanticipated benefit of World War II was the lasting effect of military training and discipline on millions of young people who returned home to the challenges of civilian life. Philip L. Cochran of Maple City, Michigan, was a Marine then and, like all Marines, remains one to this day.

As I initially reflect on my experiences in the Marine Corps during World War II, as I have so often during the past half century, I am still overwhelmed with a tremendous sense of gratitude . . . gratitude first of all that I returned home in 1946 sound in mind and body, returning a vastly different young man than the one who had left in the Fall of 1941, a much, much better person in so many ways . . . gratitude for the opportunity to be a United States Marine, a pride inculcated in all Marines from day one of their service, in my case from the moment I arrived in Quantico, Virginia in the Fall of 1941 for their Officers Training Program, a pride that will never leave me . . . once a Marine, always a Marine.

I do not recall many negatives . . . cer-

tainly great sadness over the loss of
many comrades and good friends . . .
Frank Shafer from Hinsdale, Illinois,
Reid Woodward from Leroy, New York,
Bob Cassels from Clarendon Hills, Illinois, Kenneth MacLeod from California, and when my closest friend and
fellow Marine officer, Harry Edwards,
who was like a brother to me, was killed
on Saipan, I wept openly and copiously.
I was deeply saddened, also, that I
couldn't be home to see my Dad before
he died and to help Mom with her
grief. . . .

Before the war, as the third boy in a
family of three boys and three girls,
puny and underweight, with two athlet-
ically talented older brothers, I had a
strong inferiority complex. Indeed, one
of my motivations in trying to join the
Marine Corps, "the rough and tough
foot soldiers," was to prove to my Dad
that I was as good as my older brothers.
Becoming a Marine, graduating tenth
in my class at Quantico out of 320, serving the Corps honorably and retiring as

a Major gave me a high sense of self-worth . . . not an ego trip, but just feeling good about myself, a feeling that has never left me. Without question, this sense of self-worth, which the Marine Corps gave me, has been a source of strength and well-being through my life. (Incidentally, Dad, indeed, became very proud of me. On one occasion, as Mom and Dad were entertaining at an open house in our home one Christmas Eve, as was their custom, Dad, having been slightly over-served with Tom and Jerry's, a popular Christmas season alcoholic beverage at the time, announced to the assembled guests that I had just been promoted to First Lieutenant and was in charge of all the Marines in the South Pacific!!)

During my service years, I had developed significant organizational skills, both as a staff officer in our battalion and, after returning from the South Pacific theater, on the staff of the Commandant of the Marine Corps in Washington, D.C. This experience had a substantial effect on my career after the war. Returning to my pre-war position as a salesman for a large insurance agency in Chicago, I missed being part of an organizational management and resigned as a salesman. Our chairman, Wade Fetzer, a great and wise man, refused to accept my resignation and instead offered me a job as director of recruiting and training. I became a member of his staff, and eventually became chairman and CEO of the firm, the largest private insurance agency in the Midwest, as well as a director of three New York Stock Exchange companies. . . .

I returned to civilian life in 1946 with a feeling of great debt for having been spared injury or disabling illness, with a resulting heavy sense of obligation to my family, my community and my country. Without question, this sense of obligation motivated me significantly in striving to repay the debt I believed I owed. As a consequence, I have had a lifetime of devotion to community service, in my home town, Hinsdale, Illinois, in Chicago, and, after I retired, in Glen Arbor and Traverse City, Michigan.

With all these positive impacts on my life since the war, not for an instant could I think that my service in World War II represented a sacrifice. To the contrary, my life gained so much from those experiences. I returned way ahead of the game, and I'm still ahead. I owe so much to my experiences during the war and to the United States Marine Corps.

WILLIAM "BUD" ANTHONY OF MULDROW, Oklahoma, was a child of the Depression whose life was changed by military service.

I too, have buried my memories of my life in the 40's. First, poverty, we had a dirt floor in our one room house. A man, woman and eight children. I was the oldest, and when I turned 17 years old, I enlisted in the Army. This was the first time I had more than one pair of shoes and more than two pairs of pants. I remember telling the supply sergeant, "What am I to do with all of these clothes?" He replied, "Keep moving, soldier." That was the first time anyone had called me soldier. I still think about how I swelled up with pride.

At that early age in our lives, we trusted everyone, and anyone older was "Mr. or Mrs." Respect was coveted and demanded. Trust was a part of our lives. If we were asked if we did something, we never thought of denying it. Good moral character was the only way we knew. . . .

I didn't realize we were poor until I went into the service. . . .

I know in my heart that if we hadn't gone to war, I would not have been successful at anything. President Truman saved my life. We were scheduled to go in Tokyo Bay on the 2nd wave. I feel to this day, if he hadn't dropped the bomb . . . I would have perished. Yes, I saw Hiroshima, but at that time in my life, I didn't realize what I was looking at. It just looked like nothing had been there for a thousand years. Only cement rubble and devastation. Yes, it killed thousands, but on the other side, we killed thousands and saved a lot more Americans and Japanese than the bomb killed.

I am starting to remember things I don't want to, so I will close my letter.

JOE COPPOLA OF PARAMUS, NEW JERSEY, WAS a youngster when war broke out.

I was almost 12 when Japan attacked Pearl Harbor, and my memory of that whole era is very vivid. Three of my older cousins who lived across the street joined up, as did all the other young guys in the neighborhood. I never doubted their ability to win the war because I knew no one could defeat the American soldier.

The years right after the end of the war are also quite vivid. It was difficult to walk down our main shopping avenue because of all the baby carriages. I can still see the embarrassed look on some returning veteran as he is given a spontaneous hug by an eight-months-pregnant ex-classmate. . . .

In 1980 we helped close the Westinghouse Elevator plant in Jersey City by conducting an outplacement program for their last 220 employees. Many of the men involved were World War II veterans who were employed as machinists, electrical technicians and maintenance people. They could do anything with their hands, and several had unusual hobbies. One had played the piano at Carnegie Hall, another made artistic wall creations from sheet copper, one was an artist and another owned and raced horses. I commented at the time that if I were ever marooned on an island I would like it to be with these men because they could build a city. The greatest generation was also the most capable generation. They could and did do it all.

LINDA MATTHEWS OF DOYLESTOWN, PENN-sylvania, learned lessons of life and death as a result of her father's experiences as a Marine sergeant.

My father [Walter Ciesielka] was a Marine in the Pacific Campaign and through the years, prompted by his reminiscences, I have striven to learn as much as possible about the Pacific and European Campaigns. To discuss this with my peers, however, has been a disappointment for me as I have found that many in my generation have a general sense of apathy regarding this period of history and the experiences of their parents. . . .

As for my father, he passed away ten years ago. The doctors told him that he had inoperable lung cancer with six months to live. He never discussed his illness, nor did he complain about his pain. He worked at his electrical business until two months before his death, which was three years after they told him he had six months to live.

I will always remember his strength and the one thing he told me before his death. He was in the second wave at Iwo Jima; mortar shells were hitting his unit and he jumped into a trench with four other Marines. A shell hit the trench and he was the only one to walk out alive. The way he viewed it, he could not complain about his impending death as he was given forty-five years he should not have had. . . .

I am sure there are many such stories of the common soldier who did not make it into politics, take advantage of the G.I. Bill or start major lucrative businesses. My father was a product of the depression, with both parents deceased before he was fourteen and with only a ninth grade education. His major contributions in life were to marry at eighteen, participate in a war, have two children, [and] become a policeman and later an electrician. Above all, he loved and provided for his family. If there is a sequel to your book you might want to consider dealing with the common soldier or "grunt" who did not end up with wealth or fame but was just absorbed back into the population making the best of what life doled out.

AMERICA, A NATION OF IMMIGRANTS, HAD IN its military force young men not long removed from the countries they were now expected to fight. Carole Lalli of New York City wrote about her uncle, Armand Casini, an Italian-American, and his friends.

They were architecture students at Cooper Union, and the friendship, along with many others from Cooper, was life-long. Uncle Armand served in Italy, in the Apennines, and his hand-drawn maps were used by the 10th Mountain Division. . . .

Armand always said that he and his friends, who were terrific skiers, joined the 10th Mountain Division so that they could enjoy the sport. I think they actually were dropped from planes on skis into the mountains, but Armand never talked about any heroic adventures.

The other thing that always has struck me about the war is that so many first-generation Americans were sent back to the countries from which their parents had emigrated. This too seems to have been taken in stride, which I deeply suspect would be very different for our more self-involved generation. I have a letter that Armand sent to my grandmother when he was stationed in Rome, updating her on various family members still living there; the letter has the casual tone of someone on vacation. . . .

Following the war, Armand had a marvelous career with Skidmore Owings and Merrill; he was design chief on projects around the world before he joined the San Francisco office. Years later, he was about to become a partner when everyone realized that, because he had volunteered in the middle of his final year at Cooper Union, he did not have a degree. So, at the height of his career, he spent a semester at Berkeley, which he enjoyed enormously—no whining.

HENRY KISSINGER WAS ONE OF THOUSANDS of European Jews who came to this country to escape Hitler's extermination campaign. Kissinger returned to Germany during the war as a uniformed member of the U.S. Army.

Herbert Owens of New York City escaped from Vienna in 1938. Austria had been annexed by Hitler, and Herbert's father had already spent a year in a concentration camp. Owens writes about the struggle to survive that refugees faced in New York, and the euphoria he felt on returning to Austria in 1943 as an American soldier and citizen. He told me he considers this his greatest achievement.

> I was born in Vienna, Austria, in June 1924. My father was the third-generation owner of a Drugstore in the center of town. My mother died when I was 8. I attended public school from age 6 to age 10, then entered high school, learning Latin and English.
>
> In March 1938 Hitler annexed Austria, the "Anschluss." The route into

town was down our street. I was then
not quite 14. In May 1938 most of the
Jewish Men were arrested, my father
included, and sent to Dachau Concentration Camp. I lined up at Gestapo
headquarters and was told that Hitler
wanted all Jews to leave Austria and as
soon as we found a place to go to, my
father would be released.

There were few options. Very few
countries opened their doors. Entry to
the United States was by a quota system, so I registered for a number. A
sponsor was needed. Two cousins who
themselves had just emigrated to the
United States based on an employment
contract sent us the required "Affidavit
of Support" in December 1938.

Permission to leave Austria could be
obtained only by leaving all possessions
behind. This meant dealing with financial matters about which I had very little
knowledge. Fortunately a good friend of
my father who was not Jewish helped
me, and sometime around my 15th
Birthday the exit papers were complete.

Providence shone on us when shortly thereafter I was notified by the American Consulate that our quota number had been reached, the "affidavit" [had been] accepted and a visa would be issued, subject only to a physical.

When I presented this to the Gestapo, they did approve my father's release, after he was imprisoned more than a year, with the proviso that we would leave within 60 days.

We almost didn't make it out of Vienna. On September 3, [1939,] World War II started, our passage was booked from Trieste, Italy, to New York for early November. We managed to hide out and finally left in time to get the boat, taking only one suitcase with clothes and no money.

We arrived in November and found a furnished room on the West Side. My father got a minimum wage job to deliver packages. It was not easy to make ends meet so when I was 16 I got working papers and continued High School at night. There were many other "refugees," as we were known, attending for the same reasons, including my wife who I was fortunate to meet there. She too, coincidentally, had recently come from Vienna.

On my 18th Birthday I registered for Selective Service and was called to active duty in February 1943. I was assigned to Fort Dix for basic training. The very first day we were taken to Federal Court in Newark and sworn in as Citizens of the U.S.

After completing the basic training, I was sent to the Signal Corps in Ft. Monmouth, N.J., to attend Radar school. In July 1943, now 19, my wife and I were married. After completing some preliminary courses we [soldiers] were trained by engineers from A.T.&T. to operate a new "Top Secret" Microwave communication system which they had just developed for the U.S. military.

A unit was formed and we were sent to Wiesbaden, Germany. The war in Europe ended. The cable and tele-

322 / TOM BROKAW

phone systems were totally destroyed. The Chief Signal Officer happened to come to our compound looking for personnel who spoke German. Plans were made to rehabilitate German installations somewhat similar to what we had been trained on, located on mountaintops throughout the country.

Together with another few men, I was selected and assigned to General Eisenhower's headquarters, with the task to rebuild and operate stations to carry telephone and telegraph traffic.

I interviewed prisoners of war, looking for soldiers who had operated this equipment; [I] assembled a crew, established a repair shop and our team successfully reestablished communications. My travels took me to Frankfurt, Munich, Cologne and to Vienna.

The euphoria of returning as a soldier of my new country, just six years after leaving, remains a lasting memory.

My wife and I just celebrated our 75th Birthday and our 56th Wedding Anniversary. Not a day passes without us thinking about our past and how very fortunate we are to live in freedom in the greatest country in the world.

NOT ALL OF THE VETERANS WERE ABLE TO pick up where they left off. Some were changed forever by their wounds. Terry M. Supple of Woodland Hills, California, and his family came to know the cost of war and the exceptional strength of two veterans.

During the war, Birmingham Hospital (later Birmingham High School) was built in Van Nuys, California, and it became the center for servicemen with spinal injuries. Hundreds of young men came to this facility for medical treatment. But more often, it was for rehabilitation and training in the use of devices such as wheelchairs that allowed them to return to civilian lives as paraplegics or quadriplegics. . . .

It was in this neighborhood and environment that my four brothers and I grew up. On our street in Encino were a couple of these paraplegic veterans. And in the neighborhood surrounding ours, there were several more. . . .

I finished your book while flying to Chicago on April 18th. I was saddened to learn that Randall E. "Uppy" Updyke died the following day at the Veterans Hospital in Seattle. In all respects, he was larger than life. As a young infantry lieutenant, he was seriously wounded by a land mine in Europe. As a result of his injuries, he became a paraplegic and was sent to Birmingham Hospital. While there, he met and fell in love with a young nurse named Lil. She was at his bedside as he died 54 years later.

Uppy was a very outgoing man who gained substantial girth confined to his wheelchair. He never lost the "colorful" infantry language that went well with his gregarious personality. Because of his handicap, Uppy and Lil could not have children, so instead they drew all the kids in the neighborhood to them like a magnet. With a group of 6 to 10 year olds, Uppy organized the "Gaynor

Army," named after the street where we all lived.

He became active in the Disabled American Veterans (DAV) organization in the San Fernando Valley, and was the first commander of their chapter that is still going strong. About 40 years ago, they moved to the Hood Canal area in Washington and set up a marina. Uppy became quite well known and was often visible driving his tugboat throughout the Puget Sound. About 10 years ago, he was honored as the Veteran of the Year for the State of Washington.

They had a huge impact on our family as dear friends to my parents and us. Since they couldn't have children of their own, they "adopted" my younger brother, Casey, as their own. After they moved to Washington, he would spend the summers working with them at the marina. During the Vietnam War, Casey joined the Army (just like Uppy) and served with distinction in the 101st Airborne in Vietnam. When the war was over, he remained in the Army until he retired a few years ago from Fort Lewis, Washington. He still lives in the area, and he and his wife were with Uppy and Lil when Uppy passed away. . . .

Edward L. "Shorty" Gordon was an Air Force tail gunner, shot down over Europe. His story is similar to Uppy's in that he was sent to Birmingham Hospital, where he met and married a young nurse, Jeanie. Shorty and Jeanie lived across the street from us, and like the Updykes, always enjoyed being around the neighborhood kids.

Shorty was a handsome Texan who had a wonderful upper body physique. It must have been very difficult for him to be confined to a wheelchair. It didn't stop him, however. He enjoyed shooting hoops with the kids on the driveway, and could sink a two-hand set shot from 30 feet away. He was employed in sales at a steel supply yard and got me a job driving a truck for them during my high school years.

He and Jeanie also "adopted" one of my brothers, Rory. Even after we all moved out of the neighborhood, Rory returned often for dinner . . . or to sit around for a few drinks with Shorty and some of his buddies. Both Shorty and Jeanie have passed away. But I was always struck by the love that bound the two people together, knowing as they did that once they committed to each other, it really was "for better or worse."

As I noted earlier, the group of men and their wives were wonderful to be around. Although they experienced many physical hardships, they moved on with their lives, making them as normal as possible.

IN THIS AGE OF SELF-ABSORPTION THE SELF-lessness of many veterans strikes a chord. Jonathan Birenbaum of Scarsdale, New York, described his appreciation of his father.

Having read *The Greatest Generation,* I find myself compelled to write to you. . . . I am writing to thank you for

helping me, after 45 years, to understand more fully my 85 year old father.
Your observations and commentary
have caused me to have a greater appreciation for a man I have loved and
whose life has been devoted to my sister, my mother and me in a way that I
am not sure even he has understood.

THE AMERICAN FLAG REMAINS FOR MANY
World War II veterans an almost sacred
symbol of patriotism. They have been the
primary promoters of a so far unsuccessful
campaign to make desecration of the flag
unconstitutional. Edward F. Jonat of Great
Neck, New York, became a tireless promoter
of the flag when he came home from the war
and joined the New York City fire department. His devotion to the flag never wa-
vered; neither did his sense of right and
wrong.

Like many of the people in your book, I
found the war to be a great adventure. I
found myself leaving N.Y.C. for the first

time, seeing many parts of our beautiful country and living with shipmates from many of our 48 States. That thrill I felt sailing out under the Golden Gate on a beautiful new submarine into the Pacific, China and Yellow seas. Every day presented a new challenge, thrill and experience. In the conning tower I learned leadership from my Captains that held me in good stead when I became an officer in F.D.N.Y. [the Fire Department of New York City]. . . .

In '66 and '67 I was a chief in the 4th Div.—Harlem—and facing a strange test. . . . The children at Columbia [University] were rioting and burning our flag and the N.Y.P.D. asked us to open our hose and deck pipes on them. Boy was I happy when I received the shortest and best directive I received in the F.D.N.Y. It stated, "FDNY fights fires not people."

At a Christmas party last year I was again reminded of the impact my love of our Flag had on my career when after 22 years in retirement I met an old friend of mine. He greeted me by saying, "Ed Jonat, every time your name comes up people remember the Flag."

THOSE WHO LIVED THROUGH THE DEPRESsion and World War II learned lifelong lessons in the importance of working together. As a result, later in life they became another kind of army, a formidable force of volunteers. Roderick Berry of Mount Dora, Florida, is typical.

Although I can relate somewhat to the individuals you chronicle, I never felt I was of the greatest generation. I spent 40 months overseas, mainly in Hawaii and the Ellice Islands, and I never fired a shot. Hardly arduous duty, merely maintaining radio communication. In truth I felt I was wasting my time and the government's. But I did what I was told, caused no trouble, made sergeant and some good friends.

Your book prompted me to rethink my thoughts after my generation. I began talking about it to friends about 15–20 years younger than me. You must understand, far too many of my generation have already left me. I was surprised to learn many people agreed with you and consequently disagreed with me. There is a difference among generations. Far too vividly, I remember the Depression, and serving in the army was better than what we left home. . . .

I erred when I decided not to attend college, but I made a living by working until [the age of] 74. I am in Florida for 23 years now. I volunteer in elementary school a few days a week teaching proper English, grammar, and how to write any type of letter, essay, story, etc. I work with 3rd graders who need extra attention because they are behind. I will note that this comprises about one third of the class. My reward is having some student state, "Thank you Mr. Berry, now I get it." Although I was never a hero during the war I now give back to the people of the U.S.A. In return I get even more back.

I almost forgot. I was born in England and arrived here when I was three years old, became a citizen at 24 while in the service.

Now I am proud of my generation, thanks to you, and wish I could have contributed more.

In *The Greatest Generation* I wrote about Chesterfield Smith, a World War II veteran who later became president of the American Bar Association and took a courageous stand against Richard Nixon during Watergate. His protégée Martha W. Barnett was recently elected to the ABA office her mentor once held. She will be forever grateful to him.

Let me give you just one example of how Chesterfield mentors by transferring his personal credibility. When I was a young lawyer at my first ABA convention, Chesterfield spent a great deal of time introducing me to his friends and colleagues. One afternoon, noticing, I suspect, that I had nothing better to do, he decided that I needed to meet Warren Burger, then Chief Justice of the United States Supreme Court. He introduced me by saying, "Mr. Chief, I want you to meet *my* lawyer, Martha Barnett." For many years thereafter, that is how I was known—as Chesterfield Smith's lawyer. Believe me, being known by that title makes a difference.

Many years have passed since the first ABA meeting. Following in his footsteps, I now begin my tenure as president-elect of the American Bar Association. In this role, I have the opportunity to represent the legal profession and to perpetuate the ideals exemplified by Chesterfield Smith. I have been fortunate in the past few years to receive recognition for various accomplishments. My greatest personal accolade, however, was captured a number of years ago in an article about future presidents of the American Bar Association. In talking favorably about my prospects, a reporter attributed them to the fact that I had Chesterfield Smith at my side. . . . How right he was! As blessed as I am to have Chesterfield in my life, I am but one of thousands who benefit from this remarkable man.

JULES RIEDEL OF RED HOOK, NEW YORK, wrote about his father-in-law, William (Bill) Hull, who served at Iwo Jima and recognized himself in a *Greatest Generation* picture of sailors posing in a Panama photo studio.

Bill is originally from Troy, NY, a veteran of WWII, a former Golden Gloves boxer who after being discharged from the Navy started as a janitor for and retired from Niagara-Mohawk after 35 years as a Gas Line Crew Foreman. His passions were camping, fishing and trapping and he now enjoys the quiet joy of bird-watching and the Travel Channel. A far cry from what he endured as a young man. . . .

His first wife, Eileen, had tuberculosis and died of pneumonia 8/15/56. Their daughter, Barbara Ann (my wife), was raised solely by Bill for almost six years and never had a baby-sitter. She tagged along everywhere with her father—the Irish pubs, American Legion, the non-tourist Catskill bars, etc. When Bill married Doris in 1961, the family became whole again and thrived on determination, guts, pride and a terrific sense of humor. . . .

He served aboard the USS *Jupiter,* basically a supply ship for the 5th Fleet in the Pacific Theater that prior to the war was a cargo ship named the SS *Flying Cloud.* During the war, she traveled one hundred thirty-five thousand two hundred eighteen miles, carrying thousands of tons of supplies and troops to various fronts, all of which involved crossing the equator 14 times and picking up 10 battle stars along the way. [Supply ships] were often considered the first and easy pickings for the enemy. Cutting off supplies to the other warships was considered critical and they, many times, came under greater attack than other vessels. At one point, Bill was continuously at sea for 18 months and under fire.

From what I've been able to piece together, based on documents Bill still has . . . he actively participated in twelve battles, eleven of which are described below, and was awarded the Philippine Liberation Ribbon with two Bronze Stars for bravery.

Battles William L. Hull participated in and has been officially cited for:

Guadalcanal, Solomon Islands
(enemy attack)
Tarawa, Gilbert Islands (landing operation)
Saipan, Marianas Islands (initial landings)
Palau Islands (initial landings and support-reserve force)
Leyte, Philippine Islands (initial landings)
Battle for Leyte Gulf (early phase)

Leyte, Philippine Islands (reinforce-
ment)
Dutch New Guinea (enemy air attacks)
Lingayen Gulf, Luzon, Philippine Islands (initial landings)
Iwo Jima, Kazan Retto (initial landings and disembarkation)
Okinawa Shima, Nansei Shoto (landing of supplies and equipment)

While spending time with [my in-laws]
back in June, at the cabin he and Doris
built 31 years ago in Vermont (the
American flag always flies on the
grounds), I had left the book on a
table. . . . He was browsing through it,
when suddenly he began making excla-
mations about a photo. It turns out he
is the sailor third from the left and they
had the same photo at one time.

You have no idea of how emotional it
was for him and how excited and ani-
mated he became at the discovery. For
us it seemed unbelievable, mostly because of the pure coincidence of him

just happening to pick up the book and thumbing through it. Because of his vision problems, he just looks through books with lots of photos in them. . . .

Bill is a fixture in the Albia neighborhood of Troy, NY, having been born there and then lived in the same house for over 50 years. He is recognized by all during his summer motorized wheelchair excursions throughout the neighborhood and to the American Legion, which he visits regularly. The book accompanies him on these daily trips and to anyone who is willing to try and listen, he shows the picture and proudly points to his chest saying, "Me, me . . ."

Mr. Brokaw, as a direct descendant of "the Greatest Generation" myself, I found your book to be a great inspiration and feel it should be required reading for all high schoolers. . . . It woke up a stirring of pride in a member of our family who for 13 years has not been able to express himself about his accomplishments during the horrors of battle. To begin with, he is a humble man, used to hardship, a non-complainer and like many other veterans downplays [his] role in wartime. Your book freed up emotions in him and made family members and friends aware that this man demonstrated the greatness you describe so well in your book. We thank you for that.

ONE OF THE GREAT CALIFORNIA SUCCESS stories of the postwar years involved the San Francisco–based real estate empire of Walter H. Shorenstein. He remains a major force in real estate development, Democratic party politics, and philanthropy. He credits his Army service with getting him started.

When the draft was started in 1940, President Roosevelt personally drew the numbers to select the first one hundred groups of draftees. Out of thousands of numbers, FDR chose mine on his 25th pick, and in November 1940 I joined the first group of inductees at Camp Upton, on Long Island, New York.

Even as thousands of young men descended on the place, it was clear that Camp Upton had neither the staff nor the facilities to receive us. After an abbreviated basic training, I was pulled into the Classification Section, interviewing the incoming waves of draftees and recommending assignments. The need for qualified staff was such that I remained there for my whole year of military service, and was discharged in November 1941. Just a few weeks later, I was driving into New York when I heard that Pearl Harbor had been bombed. I turned around and drove back to Camp Upton to reenlist. . . .

With classification duties reassigned, I was selected for quartermaster officer training at Camp Lee, Virginia, late in 1942. . . . We worked around the clock to get air units prepared for Operation Torch, the invasion of North Africa.

The challenges and stress that were such a big part of every day led to a huge burnout rate. For relief, the Colonel would send us to various schools for brief periods. I attended

Field Grade Officers Training, and later was selected for the Air Corps Command and General Staff School. This in-depth training, combined with the skills I was learning from my duties, gave me what I consider the equivalent of an MBA. Though I was only 26 and a first lieutenant, I had responsibilities unlike anything the civilian world could have offered. . . .

Despite the long, stressful hours, the job never really felt like work. We knew that we were accomplishing something very important. When I consider my accomplishments subsequently, I feel very well served by the discipline and analytical skills I developed in the service. Having had my endurance and resourcefulness tested under the most critical circumstances, I came away at the end of the war with the confidence and independence to make a new start in a new city with just $1000 in my pocket and a pregnant wife.

I think for many people the drive and determination that sustained them during the war carried over into their civilian lives. In my own career I have tried to operate by the same standards of achievement that were demanded of me by the service. Even more importantly, I think the strength and shared values derived from the war have set a high standard for each subsequent generation. From civil rights to technological transformation, America's younger generations have grown up with the idea that dedicated people working together can truly change the world. To me, this is the greatest and most enduring legacy that my generation has passed on.

ONE OF WORLD WAR II's LARGER-THAN-LIFE heroes was Marine fighter pilot Joe Foss, who earned the Congressional Medal of Honor for his exploits in the skies over the Pacific. When I wrote about him in *The Greatest Generation* I described the postwar years when one of his children was struggling with cerebral palsy. The following letter from William Smith, now living in

California, recounts the role Joe Foss played in the life of Smith's son, another cerebral palsy victim.

Living in Kansas City, Missouri, during the mid-forties, my wife and I learned that our three-year-old son, Billy, had cerebral palsy. We were devastated. We knew nothing about the affliction.

The United Cerebral Palsy Association invited parents to a local church to learn about the dilemma we were facing. We drove to the church one snowy Sunday evening and found only one other couple there. But soon a large man entered the room. He had flown down from South Dakota. Joe Foss. He told us about his daughter with cerebral palsy.

Although this was some fifty years ago, I still remember his words of encouragement. We left the small gathering that night with hope and feeling that we and Billy would be able to cope with the disease.

However, when he was in high school, and [during his] first year of college, we were advised by his counselors that we should not encourage Bill to go on and get a college degree. We were told the best we could expect was the possibility he could work with Good Will Industries in some manner.

Apparently some of the words of encouragement we received from Joe Foss that night in Kansas City had rubbed off on Bill. He went on to graduate and was employed by the U.S. Forest Service in their computer operation. He wrote programs that were used throughout the country and he supervised a computer office. He will complete a very successful career with the federal government in a few years.

ANOTHER VETERAN FROM THE PAGES OF *THE Greatest Generation,* California schoolteacher Luis Armijo—Army Joe, as the kids called him—inspired a number of letters of appreciation. One came from Paul H. Limon of Fullerton, California.

Dear Mr. Armijo,

Just wanted to drop you a few lines to say hello and to tell you how very proud I am to be one of your former students.

I know you probably don't remember me. I was very quiet and shy back in those days. You were my typing teacher my final year, in 1966. I truly enjoyed taking typing and you as my instructor. I always remember you as a fair and honest man. . . .

I enjoyed reading your stories in Tom Brokaw's book. Little did I know that within a year and a half of graduation, I would be in the Army and in Vietnam. As you and I know, war is a terrible thing. But it makes you really appreciate this great country of ours.

Thanks again for all you have done, for me and all the students you have touched.

God bless you and your family.

CHRISTOPHER GILLESPIE, ANOTHER VIETnam veteran, who now lives in Westport

Point, Massachusetts, has often reflected on the differences between the experiences of his parents and what he endured.

In 1942, my father was a 30-year-old classics teacher, five years into his teaching career, with one small child and me on the way. He came home from class one day and announced he was joining the Navy. In his school community, there were many young [men with] families in similar circumstances, none required to go off to war. But my father, along with many of his colleagues, felt strongly that he needed to be a part of this war, so he became a 90-day wonder at Fort Schuyler, New York. Because he stammered badly, the Navy would not let him become a ship's officer, with the difficulty of issuing orders on a bridge, I suppose. Frustrated, he asked for the next most hazardous duty, and he was assigned to the Greenland Patrol. He ended up on a support base in Greenland teaching English to other servicemen. He loved that tour and loved Greenland, sending us back

Eskimo crafts and a 45 record he had made, wishing his little family back home a Merry Christmas. . . .

My mother, her world turned completely upside down, went bravely along with these developments, and had already joined the American Red Cross Motor Corps. There she met her best friend in life, and the two of them were like naughty kids in the back of the classroom. Her circumstances were not unique. All three of her brothers went off to war, two of them [going] away for at least four years.

They all made it home eventually, and I remember as a young boy the feeling in our town, a sense of communal homecoming, reunion, getting joyfully back to normal life. I remember wounded veterans panhandling on the sidewalk, the packed Memorial Day parades and red paper poppies.

That clarity of purpose and sense of community makes my tour in Vietnam seem all the more solitary and confused. The differences between my father's war and mine are enormous—

ironic and poignant, at least to me. I find myself oddly envying my father's experience.

My mother looks back over a long, happy life punctuated by worry, waiting and wars: waiting for her father to return from the trenches of World War I France, waiting for her brothers and husband to return from World War II and waiting for me to return from Vietnam.

CERTAIN BATTLES HAVE BECOME SYMBOLIC of World War II; D-Day tops the list. It was massive, daring, and successful, a critical turning point in defeating Germany. A veteran of the Pacific theater, Frank G. Nolte of Lincoln Park, Michigan, had a memorable encounter when he finally got to Normandy.

I took advantage of the GI Bill, earned a graduate degree and went on to teach at a community college for almost 40 years. I traveled from a new home purchased on the GI Bill benefits and still live in it. No member of my family ever graduated from college [before me]. I am probably the very typical man you wrote so glowingly of.

I went to Omaha in 1988, missing D-Day by about 44 years. . . .

I sat alone on the low stone wall that separates the cemetery from the beach, filled with this tremendous emotional upheaval. Our French guide interrupted my moment and the following conversation ensued.

"Were you here then?"

"No, chère. I was in Finschhafen, New Guinea, on D-Day."

"But these men, they are your peers?"

"Yes."

"I know how you feel."

"How could you, chère? You are 25, born in Paris, and a graduate of the Sorbonne. How could you know how I feel?" Rude, maybe, but given the moment . . .

"Down the road a few kilos is another cemetery [she said "Seem a Tear ee"] where my grandfather is buried. He was shot by the Gestapo on D-Day for having a radio." Not a transceiver, just a radio.

"Then you do know."

Suddenly she said, "May I sit with you for a few minutes and hold your hand?"

I probably nodded; too far into tears to speak.

After a few minutes, she stood up and said, "The tour must move on." And then she said, "May I kiss you?"

My Lord, Mr. Brokaw, what is an emotional basket case to do? I kissed her while weeping unashamedly and with considerable enthusiasm.

Do you know the lines from Emerson? When it seemed that the Civil War was nearing and when by contemporary standards the young men seemed to be fops and weaklings, Emerson wrote:

So nigh is grandeur to our dust,
So near is God to man,
When Duty whispers low, Thou must,
The youth replies, I can.

VIII

CHILDREN

Pat Zack with her father, Paul W. Tittel, Sr., 1954.

———————•———————

Few children relate easily to the young lives of their parents. Events that precede our own births automatically fall into the category of "history," a distant time however few years have actually passed. For the baby boomers, the army of children produced by the men and women who began their families once the war was over, the disjunction between their world and the world of their parents could hardly have been greater. One represented deprivation, sacrifice, and hard-won prosperity; the other, greatly expanded opportunity and, even during Vietnam, more personal choices.

Those differences led to some historic and well-documented rifts—indeed, to a cultural revolution that since has cooled. Now, based on many of the letters I received, as the boomers grow older they also become much more aware of what their parents had endured and the legacy of their early challenges.

In watching her father care for her mother after a debilitating stroke, Janet McKeon of O'Fallon, Illinois, realized that the strength of their relationship grew out of their war experience.

As a member of the early Baby Boom generation who lived through the Vietnam years, I thought we were the group who had been wronged, with our boyfriends/husbands fighting in a faraway place in a war that nobody wanted to be a part of, and with no appreciation by others of what we went through.

Your book certainly gave me a different perspective on that. But that's not all your book did for me. It made me wonder about my own parents' participation in and life during the war. Of course I knew my dad had served and that my older sister was born during the war, but he never talked about it and I guess I was never interested enough to ask.

Sad to say, but during the past year my dad and I have had a lot of time to talk since my mother had a stroke and required constant care. I made a three-hour trip home every week to help with her care and it was during this time that he started telling me about their life during the war.

What an eye-opener these stories were to me. It was hard to believe that in all those years since the war they had never complained about those hard-ships, the separations and the fear of the bombing missions (my dad was a bombardier who flew missions out of England). I had always seen my parents as good, hardworking people but the year that we cared for my mother showed me their strength, which they obviously also had during the war years. My dad cared for her 24 hours a day, never complaining, always appreciative of the help my sisters and I gave, but never demanding or expecting it. My mother endured the helplessness and, at the end, the hopelessness with quiet dignity until she died in May. . . .

My real reason for writing to you is to urge you to use your public voice to remind members of my generation who are still lucky enough to have one or both parents alive, to listen to their stories before they are lost forever.

Mike McReaken, of Manvel, Texas, wrote to describe a similar experience:

My father passed away last year after a three-year struggle with the effects of a severe stroke. He was at home because of the love and devotion of my mother, his wife of 55 years. My dad was at Pearl Harbor on one of the few ships of the line that was able to escape the sneak attack. For many years I tried to get my dad to tell me what it was like on that Sunday morning. He never would—or could—talk about it. . . .

It was difficult to read *The Greatest Generation* without tearing up or being emotionally choked up to know of the hardships, loss, and joy that my parents' generation suffered through. After watching my mother care for Dad since the day of his stroke, I always knew it was because of her unconditional love for him, and his deep-seated fear of being placed in a nursing home. But after reading about the many others in *The Greatest Generation,* I also understand and appreciate more why my parents made the choices and decisions that they did throughout their entire lives together.

I MET PAT ZACK IN LOUISVILLE, KENTUCKY, while signing copies of *The Greatest Generation.* She wanted to tell me more about her father, Paul W. Tittel, Sr.

My father served in the 537th Quartermaster Battalion of the US Army. Among other battles and campaigns, he experienced Normandy firsthand. Apparently, his experiences there changed him forever. My father refused, or was unable, to talk about anything that happened to him, or the things that he saw, during the war. As children, we thought it would be exciting to hear about how "he alone" beat the Nazis and the Japanese. He never seemed to understand our "childish fascination" and would always grow quite serious and change the subject. [When we were] high-schoolers, looking for more insight into the history we studied, he would again become very serious, only confirming or commenting on the facts. When asked for his personal reactions, he would only say, "Just pray that you never live during a world war."

In 1984, on the 40th anniversary of D-Day, my father returned to Normandy. I was told that when he stepped onto Omaha Beach, and later, Utah Beach, he fell to the ground, shaking and sobbing like a child. Still, on his return, he would not discuss his reliving of that moment. . . .

I was born in 1950, a child during the years of rebuilding after the war, experienced adolescence throughout the turbulent 60's, established a career in the 70's, became a "boomer," and began a family of my own in the 80's, and finally, reached some level of maturity in the 90's. Throughout all those years, I never really knew or understood how my father became the great man that he was. What I did know was that he never wanted his children, or future generations, to experience what he did during the war, and did all that he could to ensure that the world, at least our world, would be a better place for us.

Throughout sixteen years of formal education and hours of independent study, none of the US history courses I took or books I read gave me the insight into the people who served in WWII as your book did. The stories told in *The Greatest Generation*, I believe, were my father's stories, the stories that he could never bring himself to tell. Their missions, their goals, their dreams, were his. Thank you for writing this book. Thank you for providing me with the opportunity to get to know my father.

THE PARENTS OF THE BABY BOOMERS ARE in their seventies and eighties; this is their twilight time. The father of Barbara Yearing of Ridgewood, New Jersey, suffers from terminal cancer.

My father was a recent graduate of the University of Illinois in 1943 when he joined the Army Air Corps. He hurriedly got married and then he and my mother traveled with gas rations from Chicago to California, where he was stationed as a meteorologist. Their experiences during that time organized their thinking and became part of our family history.

Today, my father lives a good distance away and is dying of cancer. I had been searching for some way to tell him how much I appreciated my childhood and all that he had done for me, but could not seem to find the words to tell him face-to-face. My dad, like many of the World War II era, has had a hard time with expressed feelings. He would have found it strange to be thanked for something that was for him a matter of course. That's when I stumbled upon your book and thought I might use it as a Christmas gift and also as a means to open up a discussion with him about his life and what an impact it has had on me.

The book captured for me what I have been trying to say to him for some time about the qualities exemplified by his generation, qualities that I have taken for granted all these years. Honesty, integrity, hard work, personal responsibility and perseverance were all around me and I absorbed them almost imperceptibly. Your book has also helped me to see my father as part of his generation and not so unusual in his somewhat intractable and unyielding beliefs.

So I sent my father your book with a letter that attempted to express my gratitude to him. I tried to let him know that I understood the uniqueness of his time in history and was proud of the way he had come through it all. Mostly

I thanked him for being a great father. He called me on Christmas Day to thank me for the note and to say that it "tugged at his heart." He finally heard me and we were finally able to connect in a meaningful way. Thank you for writing such a wonderful tribute to my father and others like him. Thanks to you I feel I have been able to say something important to him before he dies.

THE GRANDCHILDREN OF THE GREATEST Generation are hearing these stories of life in the thirties and forties for the first time. One of them is H. Harrison Wheeler of Village of Golf, Florida. He greatly admires his grandfather, who served in the Counterintelligence Corps.

The Greatest Generation was a recent college graduation gift from my grandparents who, it occurred to me as I progressed through the book, could have easily been among those you profiled. The day my grandparents were married,

in the late 1930's, their collective sav-
ings totaled a meager twenty dollars.
But they loved each other, and they
knew how to work. During World War
II my grandfather enlisted and, failing
an entrance exam into the Army Air
Corps because of poor eyesight, was
placed in the relatively thin ranks of
the Counterintelligence Corps . . . As I
have taken an interest in him and his
generation (thus the book was an appropriate present), he occasionally
opens up to me about the war—a topic
that unfailingly piques my curiosity. But
even with me, his namesake grandson,
he is often reticent and unwilling to discuss his Army days. They were, he says,
some of the worst days of his life, and
he has no wish to relive them.

After the war he returned home and
prospered in the restaurant business in
Buffalo and in the Northeast at large,
eventually selling his business to Del
Monte. . . . Yet despite his stupendous
financial success and his achievements
in the war (I know he was decorated in

one capacity or another), what my grandfather is most proud of are the five sons he and my grandmother raised and the subsequent families the boys established. My grandfather is the most brilliant, compassionate, reflective person I know. But, after having read your book, it seems obvious that many other grandchildren would echo my sentiment to describe their own grandparents.

THE RENEWAL OF INTEREST IN WORLD War II has prompted many schools to assign essay themes on the topic. Bessie Luttrell lives in Shepherdsville, Kentucky. Her social studies teacher, David Bock, sent a copy of an essay Bessie wrote about her grandfather, entitled "The Bravest Man I Will Never Know."

He stands firmly in the back of my mind; I will never know this man. He is who my father speaks proudly and passionately about. He is my grandfather,

Harold Wilber Luttrell, better known as Curly. He lived from March 10, 1915, to March 14, 1980.

My grandpa has been a major factor in my life, despite the fact that he died two years before I was born. Through the memories my father and my uncle have passed down to me, I feel I have a close relationship with him. This relationship was built upon my father and uncle's connection with their father, but has grown into a much deeper bond between my grandfather and me.

As I've learned more about my grandpa and his experience through World War II, it has strengthened my ability to stand up for what I believe in and never let people trample on my dreams. He taught me to have courage even under extremely harsh conditions. . . .

August 23, 1942. The Air Force sends my grandfather a telegram requesting his presence in the war. He leaves his wife and a baby daughter to proudly defend his country.

He was first stationed at the Air Force Mechanic School (bombers) in Lincoln, Nebraska. During his study at Nebraska he advanced to Ford, Michigan's Mechanic School. When he finished his training at Michigan, the Air Force placed him in Wendover, Utah's Gunner School. At each school he studied the most well-known American heavy bomber of WWII, which was known as the B-17 Flying Fortress.

The B-17 achieved fame in the daylight precision-bombing campaign over Germany in 1943, 1944, and 1945. It obtained a reputation of being capable of absorbing a large amount of battle damage and still continue to fly. B-17s dropped 640,036 tons of bombs on European targets during the war. Boeing records claim that the Fortress destroyed 23 enemy aircraft per thousand attacks. Approximately 4,750 B-17s were lost on combat missions, which is about ⅓ of all B-17s built. . . .

There were 340,000 people in the 8th Air Force, including 135,000 combat crewmen. 28,000 of them would become POW's (Prisoners of War), including Harold Luttrell, who was reported missing in the line of duty on January 11, 1944. . . .

He was taken to Dulag Luft (transit camp for airmen) in Wetzlar, Germany. The German soldiers moved him to Stalag Luft III (main camp). . . . As he walked to the camp, he saw [the] dead bodies of his fellow soldiers and [of] Jews piled along the roadside. He stayed in this prison for the remaining 17 months of the war.

After he arrived in Stalag Luft III the German soldiers took all of his clothing and threw him into a 50-ft. hole. Each hole was designed to hold one prisoner and the purpose for them was simple cruel torturing. . . . After the war was over, the German troops made the remaining prisoners march 200 miles for their freedom. . . . My grandfather made it through the march to freedom.

In August 1945 he was honorably discharged from the Air Force. He received a Silver Star for saving three of his crew members, by sharing his oxygen at 30,000 feet and keeping them alive while under heavy fire. Three Air Medals were given to my grandfather, [one] for each German fighter he shot down singlehandedly. He also received four Oak Leaf Clusters, [one] for each assisted kill (shooting down a German fighter).

When he entered the war he weighed 240 pounds, but when he returned home he only weighed 99 pounds.

His weight was not the only thing that changed during the war. He never forgot the total destruction of the bombs they dropped on the countries. He always thought of the women and children that were killed. The image of bombing the small towns always stuck in his mind.

Two statements my father remembers his dad saying were "A man who bragged about what he did in the war, did not see nothing or was never in the war." Also "I'm proud to be an American, and I love my country." He fought boldly to defend the country he loved most.

I never got the chance to meet my grandfather. He died on March 14, 1980 (four days after his birthday). . . .

I wish I could have had a chance to meet my grandfather before he passed away. He was a true hero to many people and I'll always hold a special spot in my heart for the man I'll never know.

ALLEN A. BEAUMONT OF SUN CITY CENter, Florida, sent a copy of the inscription his grandson wrote inside *The Greatest Generation.*

I am 78 years old and served in the Army Air Corps, the U.S. Air Corps and the U.S. Air Force from 1939 through 1973 in both active and reserve duty. I entered in September 1939 as a private and retired in September 1973 as a colonel.

My grandsons (3) have always been interested in my services to the country and I feel this particular note from #3 Grandson shows that there are still some offspring from the "baby boomers" who realize the importance of World War II and the results thereof.

Pop Pop & Nini—
    After going to Europe and Normandy, I think this book's title captures what we all feel about our grandparents. Thanks for giving us the world.

Love,
Richard #3

BRIAN W. HAAS OF GAINESVILLE, FLORIDA, writes about the sacrifices of his grandfather, who died when he was two years old.

I never knew my grandfather, Clarence Kennish, a World War II veteran. I was 2 years old when he died twenty-one years ago. I often imagine the conversations that we might have had. Unfortunately, as seems to be the case often, he rarely talked about the War. Neither my mom nor her sister knows much about what he did during the War in Europe.

The only remembrance I have from my grandfather is his old duffel bag. This is a treasure to me. It contains his Army-issue clothing, toiletries bag, a few pictures, and other small items. It is the only thing I have from him but I am so thankful to have it. But because of the stories you have gathered I feel like I know something more about my grandpa. By seeing the people who he likely fought along with, I can better imagine his experiences.

I wish that more Americans today would take the time to look back and see the sacrifices these great people made for our great country. Perhaps if they did, they would appreciate more the precious freedom that we enjoy. I am so proud of my grandfather; although he's been gone for over twenty years, in a way I feel that he lives on. America, the beautiful country that he was willing to give his life for, continues to go strong today. Every time our flag is raised, our national anthem sung, and freedom is enjoyed, I believe he lives on.

LISA M. PEDERSEN OF ROY, UTAH, SENT her impressions of her father and a poem she wrote as a tribute to his war years and later life. She plans to move back to the family farm in Iowa.

I sometimes find it incredible how an Iowa farm boy faced being sent off to parts unknown, to live in Times Square as he attended training, to see Frank Sinatra for a quarter, to sail across the Atlantic and have your ship rammed and limp into port, to liberate Moosburg and enter Dachau. . . . I intend to gather and document all these stories, experiences and feelings from my father this summer, not for any literary project but for my family history. . . .

I am sharing with you a poem I wrote for my dad this spring and which was read at the Memorial Day service at a small cemetery in Inwood [Iowa] by the

American Legion in front of a small group. My father is in his 80's and recuperating from a broken leg. He was very concerned about who would put the flags on the graves or raise the flags on the Avenue of Flags. It got done. And he was able to attend, sitting in the car. I share this with you as a fellow defender of the heritage of all our veterans. Thanks and if you ever are in northwest Iowa traveling Highway 182 north of Inwood and you come across Sunny Side Farm, feel free to drop on in, the coffee is always on.

He followed his orders with strength and resolve,
No challenge too great that he couldn't solve.
But war has a way of not favoring sides,
Bombs fall where they may leaving no place to hide.
No safe arms of family to help ease his pain,
No warm hand to hold as his life slipped away.

*But the comfort of buddies, one of their
    own,*
*His war finally over, 'twas time to go
    home.*

*And what of the soldier who lived to
    fight on?*
*Was it fate, was it luck, was it trust in
    his God?*
*No time for his grief or the sorrow of
    tears,*
*For his duty was battle, he must silence
    his fears.*

*He fought on through each battle,
    etched deep in his brain,*
*Memorized every town, every bridge, the
    terrain.*
*His prayer would be answered and peace
    reign again,*
*But how would he fit? For he wasn't the
    same.*

*He pledged an allegiance when battle
    was done,*
To carry the torch, the victory won.
He lived all these years upright and true,
*To be worthy of those who had paid war's
    due.*

SOME CHILDREN OF THE GREATEST GEN-eration have their own memories of the war years. John E. Smith of Soldotna, Alaska, was living in California as a young child.

My first memories are of my grandfa-ther, grandmother, aunt, and mom gath-ered around the radio at night listening to the news. Night after night this took place. No talking on my part was al-lowed as every word was listened to with a gravity I have never since felt. Some-times the broadcasts were very hard to hear, as there was a great deal of static noise. I still remember looking around at my family and seeing faces so serious that I was afraid.

Over time, I learned that my dad was in England getting ready to fight Hitler. I didn't learn until after the war exactly what he did. I did not find out from him, either; my grandmother had to tell me. My father never spoke to me in any de-tail about the war. I learned that he was part of the Red Ball Express hauling mostly fuel to Patton. He went to Eu-rope six days after D-Day as a buck sergeant and came home a battlefield-commissioned captain. After the war, the Army Air Corps became the Air Force and my father went with the Air Force.

The reason we moved to California was also for the war effort. My mother drove a wrecker for the military. My aunt and grandmother were building airplanes, and my grandfather was a tool and die maker also involved with building airplanes. One of the things that I to this day remember clearly is that I once saw a poster for Rosie the riveter and she had a blue and white hankie tied around her head. That night when my aunt came home she was wearing the same hankie around her head, and I thought the poster was of her.

I also remember shortages. My grandmother complained the most. Grandma liked to bake and the two most essential things, butter and sugar, were always in short supply. Many people also talk about gasoline being rationed, but rubber, i.e., tires, was also in short supply. My grandfather was something of a genius in repairing tires that were no good. He had built a little "vulcanizer," he called it. He would recap portions of old tires that other people said were not repairable. I remember people coming over at night with an old damaged tire asking Grandpa to please fix it, and he would.

When I was four years old I went from house to house with other kids asking people to donate any old aluminum pots or other aluminum they might have so it could be made into airplanes. . . .

I remember V-E [Day] as very confusing. My mother and aunt broke down and cried. My mother was essentially out of control and no one was able to make her stop crying. I was very scared, and everyone tried to tell me it was because she was so happy, but I could not believe this until much later when she did stop. My dad finally came home in 1946! I didn't even know him.

My father never really spoke to me (or anyone) about the war. When I asked him about his being commissioned an officer in the field, he only said that they were short of experienced men and that he was most experienced so they "appointed" him. He did not like being an officer and resigned his commission in 1946 to become a master sergeant.

My father passed away in 1972. His civilian funeral was held in Riverside, California. We then placed his flag-draped casket on a train. My mother was not in good health and could not go with him on the train. I rode with him in the baggage car to San Francisco, where he had a military burial with full honors. This is where I learned about some of what he had done in Europe. I still do not know how his fellow soldiers learned about his funeral but there were about fifteen men [there]. We spoke a little after the ceremony and they informed me of his bravery and leadership under fire. Most of these men were in tears and there was a lot of emotion displayed for a few moments. Then it was suddenly over, and they all (to a man) began to change the subject and start telling jokes. Each seemed to be embarrassed that they had spoken at all.

I will never forget that day, or those men. I have tears in my eyes now, just writing about it. Like you, I was raised by those men and women who rarely spoke of their sacrifice and heroism. Thank God they were there!

MAJOR JOHN CARY SERVED AS A FIELD surgeon in the Army, and when he came home he was chief of staff at St. Luke's Medical Center in Milwaukee. One of his sons, John M. Cary of Mequon, Wisconsin, still senses his presence and feels connected to what he went through.

Permit me to tell you about my dad, who was in the Army for 5 years and ultimately served in the Battle of the

Bulge as a field surgeon. As was the case with so many of your "heroes," Dad never talked about the war. His only comment was "Those who talk the most, did the least." . . .

He settled in Milwaukee after the War and later became chief of staff of Milwaukee's most prominent medical center. His staff meetings were brief and run without unnecessary banter, probably [as] a result of his military days. When someone would talk too long, his standard response was "Write me a letter, next question!" He saw a son return from Vietnam unaware of the psychological scars which would appear later. Another son has made a career in the Navy medical service and will retire in a year or two. He buried his oldest son [who died of] cancer following 30 years of chronic kidney disease. . . .

Since [my father's] death in 1995, I had his Bronze Star, battle ribbons, dog tags, religious medal and medical insignia framed along with his Army portrait as a 34-year-old major. They proudly hang in what was his living room and is now a room enjoyed by our family. It was an amazing feeling to read your book in that room while seeing him "look over" my shoulder.

I also enjoyed your book since I had the good fortune to meet the subject of one of your first stories, Tom Broderick. Mr. Broderick's daughter Molly married a friend, Wayne Barnett, about 10 years ago. . . . Wayne is now general manager of NBC's affiliate in New Orleans, WDSU, Channel 6.

I met Mr. and Mrs. Broderick at Wayne and Molly's wedding, and sadly a few years later at Molly's funeral, after her valiant battle with cancer. I was impressed with Mr. Broderick. I never knew the cause of his blindness. It was amazing to read about him in your book and make the connection. I read his story at midnight on a Saturday and had to wait until Monday morning to call Wayne and ask if it was in fact "that" Mr. Broderick. Wayne proudly said that it was. I have since written a note to Mr. Broderick to thank him for his service and tell him how much I enjoyed his story. . . .

I didn't intend for this letter to be so long. I think it became therapeutic for a son who misses his dad a great deal.

JENNY THARP YOUNG OF HACKENSACK, New Jersey, wrote to say that while sorting through her father's belongings after he was killed in an accident in January 1999, she and her siblings discovered documents indicating that he had been awarded two Purple Hearts and four Bronze Stars while serving in the 101st Airborne Division—honors he never mentioned to his family. They also learned that their mother had saved hundreds of letters he wrote to her during the war.

Although my sisters and brother at various intervals of our childhood would attempt to question Dad about the war, he had great difficulty talking about it.

We grew up in a household filled with books, articles and documentaries regarding the war, but could not discuss it with Dad, except for him to say, "Whatever you read or see, it was much worse." . . .

In reading your book, a memory came flooding back, of when my younger sister, 13 at the time, ran away. When the police called our home the next morning after picking her up during the Chicago riots, my dad insisted she was in her room sleeping. Upon returning home with her, he flew into a rage, telling her what could happen to a young woman unprotected. He recalled a horror from the war, as my sister and I stood speechless. He broke down into uncontrollable tears and walked away. That was the only time we saw him break down. We knew he had much hidden pain, and yet we had no clue. . . .

In closing, it is only after reading your book and after the death of our father that we are really and truly beginning to understand him. And in understanding our father, we are beginning to know ourselves a bit more. These men returning from war had a huge impact on all of our lives. I am sure that many or all of the children of these men who read your book will feel the same.

Here are three of the letters David Tharp wrote to his then sweetheart:

Somewhere in France—July 7, 1944
My Dearest Lou,
   I'd like to tell you what I got or rather what I had for my birthday, and if I live to be a hundred I'll never forget that day. I can't tell you the whole story, but my buddies and I stopped at a French home for some cider and while drinking that my partner told them (the French people) of my birthday. They made quite a fuss over it and gave me a bouquet of roses—red, white and blue—and a big red rose to put on my jacket. To top all this off, they gave me a bottle

of very special wine, which was very good and quite old. It was only about an hour that we spent there, but it will not be forgotten.

Forever yours, David

P.S. Don't call me Davie anymore. If you do, I'll get even one of these days. That isn't a threat. Happy happy.

Austria June 6, 1945
My Darling,

D-365 and still kicking. One year ago to-day I was a very scared lad. First I was mad and then I was scared then both of them. That was one day I shall never forget. I pray that in my future years I shall never live such a year as this past one has been.

I'm not giving you any hopes, but rumors are that I'll be coming home around Aug. or Sept. However, don't pin your hopes on it. That's strictly talk. So, Hon, if I should, you either have a vacation then or we'll take one.

You go right ahead and buy those pajamas, Hon. I'll try and remember what they're used for. Ha. . . .

Oh yes, I've been wanting to ask you something. Do you think you'll still want a short engagement? I might consider four or five days.

Auxerre, France
August 9, 1945

Darling, I'm so glad you feel the way you do about the racial problems of today. At least we shouldn't be fighting over that. I want my children to be brought up to feel that they are equal and not to hate people because they are black. Oh I can't really explain it here on paper, but I'm sure you know what I mean. As you said, Hon, we wouldn't have the large racial problem we have today if the parents didn't teach their children about it.

GORDON MORRIS OF LANCASTER, TEXAS, described how *The Greatest Generation* brought him closer to his father.

Dad began college with little idea of what he wanted to do in life. When the war began he enlisted and served with the Chinese army in Burma under the command of General Stilwell. Dad never talked about the war. I don't know if it was because of the horror of what he experienced, or the belief that it was simply a job to be done and done without fanfare. He went on to a career in the Army, and although there were the obvious drawbacks of moving, we gained a respect for other cultures which helps us today in our dealings with others of diverse opinion.

The following is part of a letter Morris wrote to his father.

Thank you for your hospitality during our visit. We had a great time and were glad for the opportunity to come spend time with you and Mother. I was especially glad to see how well you were able to get around and how much your health had improved.

The enclosed book is a small gift to help us commemorate Father's Day. I wish we could be with you. Although I have not read the entire book, I have read segments and heard a great deal about it. It's Tom Brokaw's chronicle of the age of America's WWII vets, your generation. It focuses on the growing up and the silent sacrifice given by the men and women of this time. It is certainly a unique and important perspective my generation seems to have misplaced. I hope you enjoy reading it. I look forward to borrowing it from you the next time we're home. I will celebrate my first Father's Day on Sunday and will think of you and give silent thanks for the direction and abilities you have passed on to me. I am, and will continue to be, forever grateful.

THERE WERE SO MANY BRANCHES OF THE main service groups that not all received the attention they deserved in *The Greatest Generation*. Thomas Uhlman of St. Petersburg, Florida, reminded me that those who served in submarines were not given much wartime credit because of censorship and their "stealth" duty in dangerous waters. In fact, 52 subs and their crews, more than 3,500 men, were lost during World War II. It was hazardous duty and heroic: American submarines were responsible for 55 percent of all Japanese vessels sunk during the war.

Many members of the Merchant Marine and their families were also disappointed that their branch of the service didn't get more attention. They reminded me that the merchant seamen who sailed into hostile waters with cargoes of vital war material were also in the service of their country and on dangerous assignments. In fact, even though more than six thousand Merchant Marine seamen lost their lives as a result of enemy action during the war, they weren't recognized as true veterans eligible for benefits until a congressional act in 1988.

By then it was too late for many of their families.

Mary C. Matranga, of San Clemente, California, wrote about her father and what he left behind after the war. As testimony to the dangers of Merchant Marine service, she also included a report on the sinking of his wartime ship, the SS *Pennmar*.

I am writing to you about my father. His name was Capt. Sigmund Charles Krolikowski. He had served on many ships. One of them was the *Pennmar*. It was sunk in the Atlantic on September 23, 1942. He later transferred to a tanker in the Pacific. At war's end he was offered [the position of] port captain of Long Beach. They needed a captain to take a tanker to Australia. While there, gas was leaking in the hold and he went down to rescue some men. He either had a gas mask on and it was defective or he did not have one on. We never got the whole story. He died saving men's lives and was buried in Australia. My mother was left with six children in ages from six months to fifteen. She did not receive any money or benefits from the government. She was about destitute. She went back to work. My sister started working at fifteen and I at 13. If my father had some benefits, life would not have been so hard. My mother and family suffered untold misery and hardship. Now after so many years they finally recognized the worth of the merchant marine. What value is it now after so many years. We couldn't engage in any activities after school and we had to work. Going through college working two jobs, working in the college to help pay for the tuition, and being restricted in extra curricular activities because of work and pressure. We could have had a normal life if he had benefits.

——————

FROM: Harold F. Spinney
3rd Officer, SS *Pennmar*
TO: Port Director, Reykjavik, Iceland
SUBJECT: Statement Regarding Loss of Two Men

I have been presently employed as the 3rd Officer of the SS *Pennmar*, having left the United States for the United Kingdom. On the 23rd of September at 21:51 the vessel was torpedoed. My usual post is #2 lifeboat, but this had been lost two days previous in a heavy gale. Therefore, I had taken command of one of the two remaining life rafts, two of these also having been lost in the storm.

After the torpedo hit, the Master ordered abandon ship. I made my way to my raft, which was on the port side of the afterdeck of the vessel. Arriving at my station I found that Harry Lane, AB Seaman, on my watch had released the tripping gear and the raft was overboard towing on its painter. There were two men on the raft, and as I stood there Lane jumped for the painter and slid down to the raft. As he did so his right leg was caught and crushed between the ship and the raft.

The vessel was still making way, and seas were breaking over the raft threatening to wash the men overboard. Two messmen, R. Gooden and Cecil Thompson, and an oiler, A. Mock, had assembled near me. I instructed them to jump over the side and swim to the raft as soon as I cut the painter. Going forward I cut the painter, and climbed back over deck cargo. I found A. Mock still on deck. I told him to jump, which he did immediately, and [I] followed at once.

The raft had by this time drifted to the ship's stern and I swam towards it. On getting aboard I had the men break out the oars and begin to get the raft away from the ship's stern as the wheel was turning over. A. Mock had made the raft and R. Gooden also, but the other man, Cecil Thompson, was still swimming for the raft. He had been calling out to us on the raft but suddenly he disappeared from sight never to be seen again.

While paddling around the starboard side of the vessel to get clear of her sinking, I suddenly saw a red life preserver, light burning, and upon bringing the raft alongside found it to be Harry Lane floating face down in the water.

He had a deep cut across the back of his head and blood was running from this cut and from his mouth. I have not the slightest doubt that he was dead. I released his body.

Rounding the bow of the ship we floated there until the ship went down and then tied the two rafts together with the #1 lifeboat.

[signed] Harold F. Spinney
3rd Officer, SS *Pennmar*

IX

·

LESSONS

John H. Chafee, USMC, 1943, following the battle of Guadalcanal.

Ozzie Sweet (extreme left, holding camera), Camp Callan, California, 1941.

Walter Morris preparing for his first jump.

————— • —————

There may never again be a time when all the layers of our complex society are so completely absorbed in a monumental challenge as they were during World War II. Everyone had a role; everyone understood that the successful outcome of the war was critical to the continuing evolution of political and personal freedom.

The nation was infused with a sense of purpose and patriotism. Political leaders, the popular culture, advertising, newspapers, and radio cheered on the war effort once the fighting began. For many young men and women, that call to duty and the constant reminders of its importance marked their lives both during the fighting and long after.

They brought home from the war fundamental lessons in the random nature of mortality, the gratification of entering into a common effort for the greater good, and the true reward of unconditional love of family. They also returned mature beyond their years, and eager to have a life of renewal and not destruction.

John Chafee, the late U.S. senator from Rhode Island who died recently at age seventy-seven, was the teenage son of a wealthy New England family when war broke out.

I had had a wonderful freshman year at Yale, going there in September 1940, and had been on the wrestling team, which greatly attracted me. I was captain, and our team was undefeated and I was undefeated. It was a big thing in my life. And the war was declared, and I was a sophomore wrestling on varsity at the time. But as deeply attached to wrestling as I was, I had no qualms about enlisting—even though I was in the ROTC and could have stayed there until I was commissioned. I decided to join the Marines, and why the Marines

I'm not quite sure. Maybe it was that they had a big poster that showed a Marine coming off the beach with a rifle over his head, saying "First to Fight—Join the Marines." I went down to the recruiting office in Providence, Rhode Island, and signed up. . . . My parents were quite enthusiastic about it. They didn't counsel against it at all.

Six months after he enlisted, Chafee was in the Pacific as a nineteen-year-old Marine private, armed with a Springfield rifle that had been designed about forty years earlier. He asked for a combat assignment and was sent to Guadalcanal as part of the invasion to secure Henderson Field, a strategically vital airstrip. Chafee was dug in when the Japanese counterattacked.

The Japanese came down with tremendous precision and sank four cruisers—three American and one Australian. They just caught us napping—they came down at full speed, at night. The Americans couldn't seem to handle things at night at that point. They switched on their lights and caught the Americans—boom boom! We were on the shore and when those big guns shoot at night, you can follow the projectiles for a while because they come out red hot. We were leaping with excitement because we thought the Americans were whipping the Japanese! And the next morning, we saw what was left of the American vessels. . . . I'll never forget the Coast Guard hauling in these Americans— the survivors—and they were just drenched with oil. You didn't have to be a Phi Beta Kappa to know that we hadn't won that battle. So it dawned on everyone that we took a beating. And particularly when we saw that our four protective vessels were gone. And the supply vessels had left because they'd be easy prey to the Japanese, and we knew that there hadn't been much time for anything to be unloaded. We're thinking, Hey—this is kind of lonely! . . .

Somebody once asked me, Did you ever think the Japanese would chase you off of Guadalcanal? It never occurred to me! I never even dreamed it, even after that! I don't know what we thought, but we weren't panicked. We just thought, Well that's today, but tomorrow's another day and the United States is not just going to leave us here.

In December, after four months at Guadalcanal, Chafee's division was sent to Australia. The following September, Chafee was selected for Officer Candidate School and returned to the United States for training at Quantico and at Fort Ritchie in Hagerstown, Maryland. On June 14, 1944, he was commissioned a second lieutenant, and then sent to Okinawa in May 1945:

There, the fighting was fierce—but by this time we had wonderful equipment. Way better than Guadalcanal . . . Okinawa was much more in the open, whereas it was more jungle fighting at Guadalcanal. It was different. I had a

small unit—my job, as part of an intel-
ligence unit, was to assess the frontline
situation and report to my superiors by
radio.

On Okinawa, Chafee went through a combat experience that gave him a perspective
on fate that guides him to this day.

I remember we were going across a rice
paddy, and they had these draining
ditches that the farmers had made and
they were very narrow, but at least it
was a ditch, maybe 12 or 14 inches
deep. We started across this open rice
paddy and got vigorously shelled by artillery. At this time, we were a rifle platoon moving forward, so there were
maybe 40 in this group. On those occasions, you want to make yourself as
small as possible and everyone tried to
squeeze into one of those ditches,
which was tough going but it made you
feel better. I was squeezed into one of
those ditches—it seemed like an eternity, but the shelling probably lasted

only 10 minutes. Afterwards, the fellow who had been in the ditch in front of me didn't get up. And I suddenly realized he was dead, he was killed from the shelling. . . . It's all luck. It just happened that I could have been the guy. I wasn't any better or braver or anything . . . it's just one of those things.

When World War II ended, Chafee went back to Yale and then on to Harvard Law School. He married and returned to Rhode Island, where he joined a prominent law firm in Providence. In 1951 he was recalled to active duty as a Marine captain in Korea. He was surprised, but, he says, "I always liked military service so it didn't bother me much to be called up."

[I] found it a great experience commanding a rifle company. It's one of those things that's unique. You're responsible for some 270 men and how you disperse them and lead them is a great experience. And you have young lieutenants working for you and you want to give them good leadership, too. It's a leadership post where you're still very close to the enlisted men. I don't think there's a better job in the Marine Corps. . . .

During World War II . . . no one needed to have explained what we were doing. Everyone understood what we were involved with. And now, with Kosovo, there was a long debate about should we be there. And back and forth it goes. Whereas there was none of that in World War II. Everyone understood.

I'm not one who believes this country is going to pot . . . or that people in my generation are of some grand status above all others. The people I work with here [in Washington] are for the most part from a younger generation. I'm 76 now and the vast majority of the people I deal with are in their middle 50s . . . and these people are terrific! And they're just as good as our generation, and I truly believe that thrown into a similar situation, they'd do just as good. . . .

After serving in Korea, Chafee returned to Rhode Island and his law practice but it wasn't long before he was active in Republican party politics in that tiny state with its long tradition of Democratic party rule. Chafee served first in the state legislature and then won three terms as governor, where he became a champion of the environment, health care, and education. After three years as secretary of the Navy during the Nixon administration, he decided to run for the U.S. Senate from Rhode Island, losing to longtime incumbent Claiborne Pell. In 1976 Chafee ran again, this time successfully, and he was elected by landslide margins in three subsequent campaigns.

Throughout his life, Chafee enjoyed an enviable reputation as a man of conviction who often found common ground between ideological opposites. He took great pride in building a consensus and getting something accomplished, especially in the areas of environmental protection and expanded health care. Shortly before his death, Chafee drew on his early years as a combat Marine to put the current Washington climate and his own life in perspective.

It's the way you approach things in life. In my case, I had my 20th birthday on Guadalcanal . . . and later I was selected for officers school . . . so you got a sense of confidence in yourself. It was very helpful because later in life, you have these challenges, and you think these guys are so bright! But then you think, I've been in the fast league and made it, and so I can make it in this league too! . . . You'd have a challenge and people would say how difficult it was. At Harvard, they'd say, Look to your left and then to your right—one of you will flunk. I thought, Look, I've been through tougher times than these. I think I'll get over *this*. So people say when you run for governor, that's so hard. But someone else has done it! I guess when you've been through a series of things in your life, you think, If I lose, I lose, what the heck. It's not like I've been shot. I just don't win. . . .

FOR THOSE WHO SURVIVED, WORLD WAR II was a gateway to opportunities they might never before have imagined. The writer Paul Fussell says bluntly, "World War II made America."

It certainly changed the life of Miguel Encinias, who grew up in the thirties in New Mexico, a difficult time and place for working-class families—especially for poor Hispanics, who were treated as second-class citizens or worse. Yet when war broke out, the Hispanic population responded with alacrity. Hispanics earned twelve Congressional Medals of Honor. Encinias wrote to tell his story of the war and its aftermath.

In 1939, at age 16, [when I was] a junior in high school, I joined a New Mexico N.G. Combat Engineers Company. I served for a year before we were federalized on September 16, 1940. I always wanted to be a fighter pilot, but I was too young, and I didn't have two years of college. In early 1942, the standards were dropped to 18 and an [intelligence] test. That April, I would be 18 years of age.

I became a Spitfire fighter pilot, and flew combat missions for nine months in Africa, Sicily and northern Italy out of Corsica. On February 19, 1944, I was shot down and wounded over a German airbase at Viterbo, [Italy,] about 100 miles north of the front line. I was captured immediately and became a POW and started my month's trip to Stalag Luft I on the Baltic coast—the only Hispanic among 10,000 officer aircrew members.

After the war, I became a charter member of the D.C. Air Guard, flying the P-47, while attending Georgetown University, from which I graduated in 1949. Just as the Korean War was nearing, I left the squadron to study at the Institut d'Etudes Politiques in Paris. The war was on when I finished my year of graduate study. I went straight to Bolling AFB, and volunteered for active duty and Korea where I flew the P-51 and later the F-86. I was shot down behind the lines and wounded on my 65th mission. We had helicopters then, and I was picked up and taken to a MASH hospital. After hospitalization elsewhere, and convalescence leave, I went back to fly 46 more missions.

When Vietnam came, I volunteered, and flew a good bit of combat missions as an advisor to Vietnamese fighter pilots.

In a later conversation, Encinias said that after he retired as a lieutenant colonel in 1971 he enrolled at the University of New Mexico, where he earned a Ph.D. in education and Spanish literature. He already had a master's degree in French from Middlebury College, courtesy of the Air Force.

Wanting to use his degrees, as he put it, "to give something back to the country and to the children," Colonel Encinias went from flying high-performance jets to a new job as a director of cross-cultural and language instruction for Albuquerque's public schools. He conducted teacher training seminars and developed performing arts activities to raise cultural awareness. In 1985 he returned to the University of New Mexico to design a curriculum more relevant to the large Hispanic student population.

During his military career, Encinias flew more than 5,000 hours and earned three Distinguished Flying Crosses, fourteen Air Medals, and two Purple Hearts.

WHEN *THE GREATEST GENERATION* WAS published, it had a striking photo on the cover—a couple standing next to a jeep, his duffel bag nearby. Their embrace appeared to be a farewell. I had several letters from couples saying it brought back memories of their own parting. Then the man who took the picture wrote. His name is Ozzie Sweet, and taking the photo launched him in a new direction: he went on to have a distinguished career as a magazine and sports photographer.

Sweet, who had worked as an extra in Hopalong Cassidy movies before enlisting, explained that he got the idea for the picture from a dog at Camp Callan in Southern California.

I took the photo when I was still in basic training, just because I thought it would be fun. It was taken with an old-time folding Kodak camera and a tripod that I borrowed. . . . The dog (which belonged to a sergeant on the base) gave me the idea. He always looked so sad, and since it was a replacement center, and G.I.s were being sent out every week, I thought it was a fitting picture.

It was the thing of shipping out— that's a sad, sad time. There wasn't the glory connected with going off to war. It was a very sad thing. And of course all the guys who did were very brave, but it wasn't a pleasant experience. So I have a special place in my heart for that photograph. . . . The soldier in the picture was a friend of mine, and the thing was finding a girl with pretty legs. I found her at a dry cleaner's place on the base. It was just putting two people together, really. I told her what I was going to do, and she was willing to do it. No model's fees then!

It was always a favorite picture, because it was my first to be published in any way. It was published in the *Range Finder*, the Camp Callan newsletter, and then in one of the newspapers in San

Diego. Then it was picked up by the picture services, and that's how it got around. . . . So when it came time to be shipped out, I was transferred instead to the Signal Corps as a PR man, and that gave me lots of opportunities to take pictures. That's where my career started. It was that photograph that kept me from being shipped out, and it was that photograph that gave me all the opportunity to take pictures. If I'd been shipped out, I might not have had the career I did.

Sweet, who now lives in New Hampshire, went on to shoot magazine cover photos of Albert Einstein, Ingrid Bergman, Helen Hayes, Grace Kelly, Dwight D. Eisenhower, John Wayne, Walt Disney, and Herbert Hoover, among others. His book on Mickey Mantle is considered a sports photography classic.

WALTER MORRIS WAS A MILITARY PIOneer AS a result of World War II: he was responsible for the formation of the first unit of black paratroopers. Morris, now retired in Florida, was a sergeant at Fort Bragg, North Carolina, with an all-black outfit. He remembers to this day the depressing effect of the worst kind of discrimination: while black soldiers were banned from the post store, Italian and German prisoners of war who had been shipped into Fort Bragg were free to use the facility.

In an interview with NBC News, Morris described how his men, who were relegated to guard duty, reacted to that egregious policy and what he decided to do about it.

You automatically develop an inferiority complex. There must be something wrong with me . . . if I can't ride in the front of the bus, and the only thing I can think of is the color of my skin, because I've gone to school. I put my pants on in the same way everyone else does. So it must be the color of my skin that causes this. And . . . when you realize that, you're in a position where you are saying[:] . . . What in the world can I do to overcome this?

. . . I saw the morale of my men at such a low ebb [that] they came off guard duty and we would go into the barracks and sleep all day. They had no initiative, and it occurred to me that as the First Sergeant of this company, I should do something about the low morale. And the idea [came to me that] to imitate the white parachute students going through their calisthenics might be one way of uplifting our men.

So we started at four o'clock every afternoon. When the white students would march off the field, the black students would march on the field.

What Morris didn't know at the time is that in Washington, black leaders such as A. Philip Randolph and Roy Wilkins were putting pressure on President Roosevelt to develop a black paratroop outfit.

At Fort Bragg, the commanding officer called Morris in and told him he would be the first member of what became a discrete unit, the 555th Parachute Infantry Battalion. Morris led a platoon of sixteen fellow Negroes, the term used then, who successfully completed their parachute training. The platoon came to be known as the Sweet Sixteen. Morris remembers their first jump.

A lot of butterflies. A lot of anxiety. We were scared to death. But we couldn't show it because the whole world had their eyes on us and they were betting that we would not jump out of any airplane in flight. And we had to prove that we could do it.

The worst-looking jump I have ever seen was our first jump. We were trained to jump with the proper attitude, which was knees together, slightly bent, the feet together, arms tight, held. And when I look at the first jump we made, I have to laugh because it was nothing like the training we received. But it was improved; by the time we got to our fourth jump, we were looking pretty good. But we came out of the plane fast.

We realized now that we were soldiers. Not guard duty soldiers, not servants, not cooks. We were actually training for combat. We were going to be paratroopers. And that . . . gave us all incentive to succeed.

The Sweet Sixteen were ready for combat. They received additional training in California and they were sure they were headed to the Pacific and the closing days of the war against Japan. Instead, with no advance warning, they were sent to the Pacific Northwest as smoke jumpers, to fight forest fires started by Japanese incendiary balloons.

Morris was deeply disappointed. As he prepared to jump into a fire in Washington State, he asked himself why he was doing this, and then he found the answer:

It occurred to me that the reason I was doing it is because of my children and my children's children. And I knew I had in my heart that . . . , this country, as great as it is, would overcome the stigma of separation and prejudice, and of course, we've come so long a ways from [the] 1945 era. And of course we have a long ways to go. But I can see the light.

I'm seventy-eight years old now and I can see the light at the end of this tunnel.

Morris has special respect for General James Gavin, the scholarly and heroic commander of the 82nd Airborne, who led the Allied forces into Germany. When Gavin returned to Fort Bragg after the war and learned that the 555th Parachute Infantry Battalion was a segregated outfit, he had it disbanded and folded into the 82nd Airborne. When Morris and his fellow pioneers from the 555th hold reunions now, they always invite General Gavin's daughter.

In 1946 Walter Morris left the Army to return home to Seattle and learn his trade from his father, a bricklayer. Morris brought those skills to New York, where he became one of the first African Americans in the bricklayers' union. He worked steadily on New York area construction projects until his retirement as superintendent of the Bedford-Stuyvesant Restoration Project in 1983.

One of his daughters is a law professor at Howard University and the other is a health department worker. He has a grandchild in the U.S. Army. How does Morris see his legacy as the first black military paratrooper?

That we succeeded where we were not expected to succeed. And we overcame the pitfalls that were put there. We overcame. And it's a warm feeling to know that, that color has nothing to do with it. It's what's in one's heart. One's spirit. And that . . . should be a lesson to all of us. We should have, and we will have, a colorless society one day. And that will be the crowning jewel in this great country's history.

THE CLOSING DAYS OF THE TWENTIETH century and the renewed interest in the World War II era have prompted many veterans to revisit the early impressions of life they described in letters home. Kay Voss, a retired businessman in Michigan, wrote the following:

Let me start by saying that I am a part of the WWII generation. I served in the Eighth Air Force as a co-pilot on a B-17, flying 31 missions.

We came home to forget what hell we had gone through and we all wanted to just get married, settle down and live like "normal" people. I arrived home on Labor Day 1945, and was at work at my old job the very next day at 8:00 A.M. My father had a grocery and meat market in which I had worked from the age of 12. He and Mother had a rough time while the war was on. Help was hard to find, rationing, customers sometimes difficult to please when you didn't have what they wanted. Dad was more than happy to have me back.

I can still remember how I felt those first few days. I was HOME!! All of those horrible days were behind me, and I was still alive!! Anyone would have had to experience that to really know what I mean.

I married my sweetheart shortly after and raised four wonderful children, two

boys and two girls. The war was all behind me and as far out of my mind as I
could put it.

It wasn't until my parents had both
passed away, and we cleaned out their
attic, that I began to think much about
my Eighth Air Force days. For in a box,
all bundled neatly according to date, I
found every letter I had ever written to
my folks clear through college and my
three years or so in service . . . several
hundred of them.

The last of those letters reflect the euphoric
relief and joy servicemen and women everywhere must have felt in the summer of
1945:

*HURRAH!! HURRAH!! I'm COMING
HOME!!!* I may not be able to write
again for a few days, so if my letters are
rather scarce from now on for a while
you'll know why. I have lots to do and
little time to do it. I haven't even started
to pack. Everything is A-OK. All of us
are so happy we can hardly keep our

feet on the ground. I am going to cut this short. Hope you'll forgive. *SEE YOU REAL SOON!!*

Excerpts from my May 21st letter:

Our time is completely our own. We have been doing absolutely nothing. I'm putting on the weight I lost last winter when we were doing all the flying. My pants almost fit again!

So, I have quite a bank roll back there now, eh Dad? Well, it's not nearly as big as it will be before I'm home again for good. There ought to be a nice little nest egg waiting for me. I don't know if I'll buy a plane or not. Right now, I have all the flying I want for a while. I'm going to be content to keep my feet on the SOLID GROUND!! Right now I have too many bad memories of things that have happened up there. Of course, civilian flying will be a lot different. I'll wait to see how I feel when I get home for good! And besides, I don't want to spend all my money on a plane . . . I've got to start thinking about settling down!

Voss eventually took over his father's grocery business, and he stayed in that line of work until he retired in 1982. In his letter to me he concluded with this passage:

> I remember the chapel service we attended just before our first mission. The chaplain prayed for our safe return, and the last song we sang, "Be Still, My Soul," returned to me many, many times in the uncertain days of combat. There seemed to be someone singing it to me. I liked to think it was my mother—and she still does, from her Heavenly Choir.

BE STILL, MY SOUL; THE LORD IS ON THY SIDE.
BEAR PATIENTLY THE CROSS OF GRIEF OR PAIN.
LEAVE TO THY GOD TO ORDER AND PROVIDE;
IN EVERY CHANGE, HE FAITHFUL WILL
REMAIN.
BE STILL, MY SOUL; THY BEST, THY
HEAVENLY FRIEND
THROUGH THORNY WAYS LEADS TO A
JOYFUL END.

BE STILL, MY SOUL; THY GOD DOTH
UNDERTAKE
TO GUIDE THE FUTURE, AS HE HAS THE PAST.
THY HOPE, THY CONFIDENCE, LET
NOTHING SHAKE;
ALL NOW MYSTERIOUS SHALL BE BRIGHT
AT LAST.
BE STILL, MY SOUL; THE WAVES AND WINDS
STILL KNOW
HIS VOICE WHO RULED THEM WHILE HE
DWELT BELOW.

BE STILL, MY SOUL; THE HOUR IS
HASTENING ON
WHEN WE SHALL BE FOREVER WITH
THE LORD,
WHEN DISAPPOINTMENT, GRIEF, AND FEAR
ARE GONE,
SORROW FORGOT, LOVE'S PUREST JOYS
RESTORED.
BE STILL, MY SOUL; WHEN CHANGE AND
TEARS ARE PAST,
ALL SAFE AND BLESSED WE SHALL MEET
AT LAST.

CONCLUSION

This has been a deeply satisfying personal journey for me. Reading the letters, hearing the stories, and sharing the emotional themes was a familial experience, intimate and nurturing. In this age of electronic communication overload, there is something reassuring and eloquent about a single voice speaking in direct, honest, and sometimes painful fashion about a passage when time was measured day by difficult day.

In a time of conspicuous self-indulgence, it is comforting to be absorbed in the lives of others who are selfless and grateful for whatever they have. Even those who were unhappy with oversights in *The Greatest Generation* made their points quietly and respectfully.

As a final note I have chosen two different stories. One came to me while I was signing books in Big Timber, Montana, a favorite small town hard by the Yellowstone River. Betty Van Mullem gave me the letters her grandparents wrote to her uncles—their sons—Raymond and James Todd on the day the Japanese surrendered. Harry Todd and his wife, Millie, in their western hamlet spoke for America.

The first letter is from Harry, who was treasurer of Golden County, Montana.

Dear Boys,

My emotions are so mixed, mingled with gladness and sadness, that I hardly know what to say to you tonight. All afternoon we gathered about the radio in the sheriff's office about every quarter hour. Finally about 3:30 P.M. National Broadcasting Co. picked up Max Jordan at Berne, Switzerland, who said the text of Japan's reply was on the way to Washington and we should have it in two hours. Talk about sweating it out— I smoked more cigarettes in the past 24 hours than I usually do in three days.

Mom and I are so happy tonight it's no use trying to tell you why and a lot of stuff like that but to be able to look forward to the time you are home again and to be sure you are coming home, well it just almost overwhelms me. I just feel like getting out the Remington and burning up all the skeet shells you brought home, Jim. This little town has very few methods of making noise but the fire bell and the Methodist church bell have rung out and the sheriff went about town sounding his siren. The Governor has proclaimed tomorrow and Thursday as holidays and the President has designated Wednesday and Thursday for all government people as holidays. Stan called us up at about 5:30 A.M. this morning to tell us the war was over. However, it was announced from the White House at 5:00 P.M. (Mountain Time) today. . . .

From now on I am going to check off the days and weeks till you get home.

Love,
Dad

Their mother, Millie, was equally relieved and joyful:

> O Darling—you will never know how happy your Dad and Mother are tonight. The past four days have been such a tense—nervewracking time. We have been having [the] radio on constantly day and night and it seemed the news would never come. Papa and I are so thankful tonight that Our Heavenly Father has spared our loved ones . . . and hope and pray they may be coming home to us soon. We do have so much to be thankful for—Raymond—that our family circle has not been broken, and how we pray you may be under the home roof soon. And while we are rejoicing—we cannot forget those who have loved ones *who will not be coming* home. There are many sorrowing broken hearts tonight—while we are rejoicing. There are so many broken homes, may God comfort these broken hearts. There are many who have made the supreme sacrifice so that we have

these happy homes of ours. To them we owe much of our freedom.

Love from Mother

The final letter—and the final word—is from Ruth Chamberlain, the grandmother of Jeremy Brunaccioni of Greenfield, Massachusetts. He sent the letter she wrote to her children on July 4, 1991. It is typical of the experiences of young couples across the nation and the tone is also characteristic of the generation. It is quietly matter-of-fact and, at the end, devoid of self-pity.

She describes her romance with Roland, her husband, from the moment they met on an ice skating rink as teenagers. He had dropped out of school at the age of sixteen to work in a shoe factory to help support his family. They went to a movie on December 7, 1941, in Manchester, New Hampshire.

Sunday was movie night and we were sitting in the State Theater on Elm Street, when the news of Pearl Harbor was flashed on the screen. I don't think there was a sound in the theater as all the uniformed men in there quietly arose and left to report to their posts. The inevitable had arrived—we were at war. . . .

We were married the next spring—1942—and Dad managed to be home till Feb. 22, 1943. By then I was pregnant 6 mos. and heartbroken when we saw him off at the train station. . . .

It was about 6 wks before I heard from him and learned he was at Camp Bliss in Texas near Austin for basic training. He was in the 365th Field Artillery Battalion attached to the 97th Infantry Div. To this day, his Serial #, 31266957, rolls readily from my lips. I wrote every day for 3 yrs except when having Nancy or the few times I saw him. . . .

In January of '44 he was stationed at Ft. Leonard Wood in Missouri and I could visit him there. . . .

When Dad thought he'd be stationed there, I returned home for Nancy. We went back out in April on an old train with wooden seats. Lots of standing room only, but a crazy young girl with an 11 mo. old baby got preferred treatment. It took several days, sitting there with a baby to bottle feed and change. And remember, no Pampers. I'll never figure out how I did it. Dumb and dumb luck! . . .

Had to wash all our clothes by hand. What diapers! Somehow managed all that alone—got all the laundry on the line and the clothesline broke dropping everything into the red clay dirt of Missouri!

Dad made Staff Sgt. and I was so proud. He was slated to go to OCS—Officer Candidate School—but by that time the war was getting worse with Japan and in June we had to come home because the outfit was going to California. . . .

They were shipped to Camp San Luis Obispo, California, and outfitted with hot weather gear. By then, the Battle of the Bulge in Belgium was waging and they were needed in Europe instead. It's a wonder we won the war!

So back they came to the East Coast in Jan. '45 and headed for a brief stop in England and then to Le Havre, France. . . .

By 1945, the Germans were really on the run, and Gen. Patton was chasing them right on to Berlin. The 97th was attached to his outfit, so Dad followed in his wake. . . .

Then came unconditional surrender in May 1945 and Alice and I celebrated on Elm St. with thousands of others. What joy!

We still had Japan to contend with, so he ended up in Bremmerton, Washington, and boarded a ship for Japan. The day they sailed, Japan also surrendered, but of course the ship sailed on. . . .

In February of 1946, exactly 3 years after being called, he returned home for good. There was a time of getting reacquainted and readjusted to a normal way of life.

A whole chunk of three years out of [our] lives and apart!

So ends the saga—any questions?

Mom

ABOUT THE AUTHOR

TOM BROKAW, a native of South Dakota, graduated from the University of South Dakota with a degree in political science. He began his journalism career in Omaha and Atlanta before joining NBC News in 1966. Brokaw was the White House correspondent for NBC News during Watergate, and from 1976 to 1981 he anchored *Today* on NBC. He has been the sole anchor and managing editor of *NBC Nightly News with Tom Brokaw* since 1983. Brokaw has won every major award in broadcast journalism, including two DuPonts, a Peabody Award, and several Emmys. He lives in New York and Montana.